Doing
Business
in China

PRAISE FOR

Doing Business in China

"Ted Plafker knows the success stories—and also the colossal failures—that have characterized the foreign presence since China's doors reopened for business in the 1980s. Twenty years of struggling, negotiating, and [living] with the Chinese have given him tremendous insight into how they think and do business, and the reader is the happy beneficiary of this wealth of knowledge."

—Scott D. Seligman, author of
Chinese Business Etiquette

"A well-balanced and practical introduction to the business environment in the fastest-growing market in the world today... Should be essential reading for any company planning to do business in China."

—Patrick Powers, vice president,
China Mundoro Mining

"An easygoing, capable guide... should be kept on the shelf close to eye level and thumbed through every time you need to understand anything from project finance to business etiquette."

—Anne Stevenson-Yang,
China Internet entrepreneur

Doing Business in China

How to Profit in the World's
Fastest Growing Market

TED PLAFKER

WARNER
BUSINESS
BOOKS ™

NEW YORK • BOSTON

Table 4.1, on page 138, appears courtesy of Erwin Sanft and Raymond Ma of BNP Paribas Peregrine. Used by permission.

The information in this book is as up-to-date as possible, however, it is sold with the understanding that legal information is often subject to new and changing interpretations, government rulings, and legislation. The reader should consult with a legal professional regarding specific questions.

Warner Business Books
Hachette Book Group USA
237 Park Avenue
New York, NY 10169
Visit our Web site at www.HachetteBookGroupUSA.com.

Originally published in hardcover by
Warner Business Books, an imprint of Warner Books.

Warner Business Books is a trademark of Time Warner Inc. or an affiliated company. Used under license by Hachette Book Group USA, which is not affiliated with Time Warner Inc.

Printed in the United States of America

First International Trade Edition: July 2007

10 9 8 7 6 5 4 3 2

ISBN 978-0-446-69863-4 (pbk.)

For Benjamin, Daniel, and Jonathan:
Beijing's youngest "old China hands."

And for Roberta, of course, who knows more than I
ever will—about doing business in China,
and about anything else that matters.

Contents

Introduction

How This Book Helps You Identify and Pursue the Top Business Opportunities in China's Emerging Market

So...you're thinking of doing business in China. For years now, you've been reading all the hype about China's rapid growth, its voracious appetite for investment, technology, commodities, goods, and services. You've been hearing one breathless account after another about Chinese industry's steady rise up the value chain, and its steady march into global markets. The dragon is roaring, the giant is awakening, and the world is trembling with awe, just as Napoleon (perhaps apocryphally) predicted two centuries ago. Add it all up, and the conclusion seems inescapable: Any company, whatever its size and whatever its business, *simply must get into China*.

If you've bothered to pick up this book, there is a fair chance you have already reached that conclusion yourself. But are you right? Do you really *need* to be in China?

Even if you've already worked this question hard and decided that your answer is yes, you may still have some nagging fears that you're simply falling victim to a herd mentality. Doesn't it seem that everyone these days is joining in a mad rush to China? And isn't it usually better to buck the trend? After all, don't the real winners look to see where the herd is moving—then cut the other way?

Sometimes they do and sometimes, of course, that's the shrewd move. Very often, though, the herd is moving so fast because it's on to something big. Clearly, that is the case with the China boom. A look at any indicator you choose, whether it's economic growth rates, consumption patterns, trade volumes, or investment figures, is enough to tell you that business in China is big and growing fast.

But size isn't everything, and just because something is big doesn't mean it is right for everyone. Among the most common pitfalls plaguing foreign businesses in China is a tendency to make sweeping generalizations, and this is one you'll have to watch out for every step of the way—starting with that very first big decision about whether you really need to be in China at all.

So what are the issues and the factors you need to consider? Yes, China is growing, and yes, China is moving fast. And yes, there probably are great opportunities for your firm to source your goods, sell your products, or promote your services in this fastest growing of markets. But despite all that, the final decision is no slam dunk, and the easy answer—"Yes, we have to be there!"—is simply not right for everyone.

Given its forbidding business climate, its uniquely complex social, legal, and political environment, and its rampant corruption, China is tough going. Setting up is costly, and progress is usually slow. In many cases, progress—not to mention profitability—is downright elusive. As many foreign companies have already proven, success in China is possible, but only for those who have the patience, persistence, and resources to see it through. It does not come on the quick, or on the cheap.

In virtually all cases, the companies that have succeeded in China first spent long years laying the groundwork and spending money rather than earning it. The conventional wisdom among some consultants is that China is only right for companies with at least $20 to $30 million in annual sales, and a workforce of at least two hundred employees. Of course, such broad and facile guidelines cannot be right for everyone, and you will need to make your own calculations based on what you yourself know about your company and your industry. But no matter what, this is where you need to start, right here with "Item Number One" on the list of things you need to know before you take the plunge: If you don't have the time and money to do it right, China is not for you.

With that, you may just decide to close this book right here. But not so fast! Even if you do not plan to do business in China yourself, it is still worth your while to understand what is going on there. Because no matter what business you do, and no matter where you do it, there is a good chance that China—on some level, directly or indirectly—is impacting your bottom line. And if it isn't yet, it probably will be soon.

Chinese demand is a key factor driving up global prices on many vital commodities, including oil, copper, coal, iron ore, and others. And strong Chinese supply is keeping the lid on the prices of other commodities, such as magnesium and rare earth metals.

As a major manufacturing and trading hub, China is also reshaping global pricing structures across a huge range of products. In chapter 6, you will see how China—using its vast supply of cheap labor, but also other competitive advantages— is undercutting competitors and taking a dominant share in markets worldwide. In many instances, it is competing against American businesses, and winning. Even when that is not the case, China is affecting markets in every part of the world and transforming the playing field of global trade.

So whether you planned on it or not, and whether you realize it yet or not, there is a good chance that what is now happening in China matters to you and your business.

If you are still thinking of doing business in China, if you have done the math and determined that you have the resources necessary to do it well, you are right to be enthusiastic about your prospects. But you also need to keep clearheaded.

The hardened China veterans, the foreigners who have already been on the ground doing business for twenty years or more, are all too familiar with a certain kind of stock character: the wide-eyed first-time visitor from the home office. One of the colorful terms they use to describe such people is *China drunk*.

They are usually easy to spot. Fresh off the plane from corporate headquarters, they are immediately dazzled by what they see. Their first stop is likely to be the gleaming new airport terminals of either Beijing or Shanghai, followed by a trip into town along a world-class freeway.

Their airport limo is likely as not to be a made-in-China Audi or deluxe Buick sedan, and as it reaches town, it will carry them past huge new buildings and bustling busy streets. The sight of so many restaurants and shops filled with so many well-dressed people will immediately reassure them that this is indeed the place to be.

The limo will then deposit them at a five-star hotel, opulently decorated with marble, dripping with glitz, and full of still more well-dressed locals talking business on their cell phones as they enjoy the high life in the lobby bar.

This kind of scene truly can be intoxicating. But just like the kick of the fiery grain liquor offered at any Chinese banquet, it can sneak up on you and knock you for a loop, leaving you with nothing but a nasty headache, a fuzzy collection of bad memories, and some gut-wrenching questions about where all your money went.

If sipped carefully, though, it can instead be enjoyed. All that marble and neon, and all that buzz are real enough, after all, and there is no reason not to allow yourself to get a little bit "China tipsy" on the potential of it all.

In fact, the very enthusiasm of these foreign executives—the bingers and the sippers alike—gives China another valuable advantage over other potentially exciting emerging markets. I would stop short of calling it a self-fulfilling prophecy, but it is fair to say that the near-universal foreign perception of China's importance does bestow important benefits.

Depending on what business you're in, you could easily make a plausible case for your company's need to be in, say, Indonesia. With its huge population, rapid modernization, and vast natural resources, Indonesia seems like a good candidate for your attention, and perhaps for your investment dollars as well. Sure, it has some of the same problems and same risks as other emerging markets, such as endemic corruption and the ever-present possibility of political or financial instability. China has these, too.

But to understand the difference, ask yourself this simple question: How many major multinationals believe Indonesia is central to their future? It may be an attractive potential market, filled with risk but also lots of upside. And maybe after checking it out, you'll actually make a move there. But if things start to go sour—if the corruption grows insurmountable, or the politics get too volatile—it will likewise be an easy decision to jump ship. The obvious conclusion: Your Indonesia play was a nice idea but in the end not worth the trouble.

In China, though, that logic simply does not apply. Many of the world's largest companies have determined—almost certainly correctly—that China is and will remain key to their long-term global plans and strategies. For better or worse, they will need to be in China, and many of them have made such massive investments that walking away is no longer an option.

This fact alone gives China a valuable built-in cushion. Because so many companies believe this to be the case, and have acted on it, they are in China and plan to stay. China thus enjoys a solid baseline influx of capital, technology, and management expertise.

If you are planning to be part of that influx, this book will arm you with the information you need to understand this nation and maximize your chances of success. There are already plenty of worthwhile books out there that can tell you where China has come from, and how it got to where it is today. Plenty of others try to fathom "what it all means." Still others make a brave attempt to predict the future of China and its place in the world. They run the gamut from Gordon G. Chang's *The Coming Collapse of China* to Ted C. Fishman's *China, Inc.: How the Rise of the Next Superpower Challenges America and the World*. The titles pretty much say it all.

The goal of this book is rather different. Working on the baseline assumption that China is and will remain important to global business, it takes the next step by explaining in a much more concise, specific, and user-friendly way how to identify and pursue the top business opportunities in this emerging market, and how to avoid the many pitfalls. Where necessary, it will also take the time to spell out some of the relevant background you'll need to get your bearings.

With China's rising profile, there is of course no shortage of quick tips, "expert" advice, and so-called surefire keys to success. Unfortunately, a lot of that has come from people who are quick to boast about how many trips they have made to China, and much of what they have to offer fails to pass the smell test.

The people who know best what they're doing here long ago stopped counting their trips. China is where they live and work. It's what they know, and it's what they do. I've drawn heavily on the wisdom of such people, as well as my own eighteen years of living and working in China, reporting on issues big and small, and chronicling the vast changes that have taken place.

You certainly won't find any magic keys to easy money or instant success, but you will find my best effort to distill my experience and understanding into vital and practical information you can use to give yourself the best odds of doing business with China smoothly, successfully, and profitably.

1

*

The Eight Greatest Business Opportunities—Pinpointing the Top Emerging Markets

With all you've read and all you've heard about the China boom, you might be tempted to think you could just show up in Beijing or Shanghai, pick a sector, hang a shingle, and start turning over deals. And true enough, business is booming across a wide variety of industries in China.

For just about any commodity or product or service you can think of, you can dig up numbers that show jaw-dropping growth in recent years. And even after weeding out all the most breathless and overstated predictions about China's prospects, you will still be left with plenty of confident—and perfectly plausible—predictions of sustained growth for the foreseeable future.

In short, while the China boom is sometimes the subject of exaggerated hype, it is not a fiction. For a few examples of the kind of attention-getting raw numbers you sometimes encounter, consider these:

- China recently budgeted for the installation of eighty-one gigawatts of new electrical generating capacity in a single year. This addition to China's existing grid *is more than the entire installed generating capacity of the United Kingdom.*

- After rising by 18 percent in 2005, the number of Chinese Internet users rose an additional 23 percent in 2006. By early 2006, it had surpassed 137 million. That's well more than the *entire population of Japan,* and about the same as the *combined populations of France and Egypt.* Yet it still represents a penetration rate of just 10.5 percent.

- And for some truly mind-blowing numbers, how about these: China already has 461 million cell phone subscribers. The customers of just one carrier, China Mobile, paid good money to send *some 203 billion short text messages in the first half of 2006.*

- If you think it's just high-tech, you're mistaken. In 2005, China's chemical fertilizer industry saw a 64 percent surge in profits. Chinese imports from Brazil of the humble soybean have *increased more than 10,000 percent in the last decade.*

Upon seeing these sorts of numbers—and there are plenty more like them—it can be easy to lose perspective. But apart from the sheer size and growth rate of any given sector, there are other things that you need to take into account. Some sectors are already relatively mature, leaving little space or market share for new entrants. In other mature sectors, entry is wide open, but cutthroat price wars pose a constant—and for some players insurmountable—threat to profitability.

In other areas, barriers explicitly work to the disadvantage of foreign firms. This is despite the sweeping open-market commitments China made when, after more than a decade of painstaking multilateral negotiations, it finally joined the World Trade Organization (WTO) at the end of 2001.

In retailing, for example, China has largely honored its commitments at the national level to allow foreign firms to open stores anywhere they choose. But many local authorities maintain their own planning and development policies, and can throw up vague or arbitrary restrictions of their own.

Foreign companies in other sectors will have difficulty gaining a foothold not because of explicit discriminatory barriers to entry, but because the lay of the land simply favors local competitors. Through their connections to local bureaucrats, Chinese firms often enjoy huge advantages in their access to land, bank credit, or even scarce supplies of power and water.

Obstacles can also emerge in what the government regards as strategically sensitive sectors. The best example of this may be telecoms. Driven by security concerns over this vital element of national infrastructure, the government has been slow to throw things open to the market and scale back its regulatory supervision of telecoms. As a result, the industry's nominal regulators remain very much involved in business operations themselves, leaving other firms, whether Chinese or foreign, in the unenviable position of trying to compete with the same bureaucrats who control their fate.

THE BEST AND BRIGHTEST

This chapter outlines eight of the sectors with the highest potential in China—ones that look certain to show continued growth, and that also have a demonstrated capacity for profitable foreign participation. Some of the industries listed here, such as telecoms and media, do suffer from the drawbacks already described. Given their size and upside potential, however, they make the grade anyway.

There are likewise plenty of moneymaking opportunities in other areas. Agricultural and food products could easily have made the list. Educational services are booming, as are travel and tourism. In these areas and many, many others, foreign players can access significant competitive advantages over local rivals and sell successfully in the vast China market. Nor is there any shortage of areas in which foreign businesses can come to China and achieve significant cost reductions in their supply or processing operations.

Some of the issues covered here in the context of one industry also apply in others. One example is the section on biotech, which discusses some of the pros and cons related to moving R&D operations to China. Many of those same considerations are equally relevant to anyone weighing such a decision in the chemical or IT industries.

Two other sectors—retailing and manufacturing—are among those with the greatest potential of all. But since they are covered in considerable depth in chapter 4, "Sales and Marketing," and chapter 6, "The China Price," respectively, there is no need to include them here.

Taken together, these sectors cover the vast bulk of the China business scene. So whether or not your business falls directly within their scope, it will be well worth your while to learn more about them, and about the unique peculiarities— be they bright spots or pitfalls—of each one.

Lastly, though it should hardly need saying, let's say it anyway: None of the areas listed here is a guaranteed gold mine. Plenty of foreign companies have already tried and failed in each. But they do represent eight of the biggest opportunities that foreign companies can exploit *if* they are properly positioned to begin with, and *if* they go about it in the right way: carefully, rationally, and forearmed with the necessary knowledge and understanding.

1. The automotive sector
2. The biotech and medical sector
3. The chemical sector
4. The construction and infrastructure sector
5. The energy sector
6. The finance sector
7. The IT/telecoms sector
8. The media and entertainment sector

Start Your Engines: The Automotive Sector

It is hard to think of another sector that has had as great an impact on China—for better and for worse—than the automotive industry. Ribbons of new superhighway now crisscross the land, and hordes of passenger cars clog the streets of Chinese cities (while their exhaust fumes, of course, clog the air).

Car ownership has become a common dream of China's emerging middle class. Whether in glitzy downtown showrooms or vast open-air car markets on the edge of town, you can watch the seduction happening up close as newly prosperous Chinese families wander around admiring the lines, kicking the tires, checking out the interiors, and leafing through the glossy brochures. Chinese yuppies are discovering both the hassles of urban commuting and the joys of weekend road-tripping. The once ubiquitous bicycle is going out of style, and the once unimaginable fast-food drive-through window is coming in. In short, "car culture" is now in full blossom in China, presenting foreign business with enormous opportunities.

Many Westerners—all too familiar with the dark side of car culture—have wondered why China would choose this path. Rather than make the same mistakes that so many other countries have made, wouldn't China be better off investing in mass transit instead of highways? Wouldn't cities (and waistlines) across China be better off if people were encouraged to keep biking, as they had been doing for decades? Seeing how their embrace of the car has led so many developed countries to oil dependency, polluted skies, and urban sprawl, why would China want to follow suit?

Well, the central government had its reasons, and it had a plan. These policy makers understood perfectly well that the advent of the car would transform China's landscape. But they also knew it had the power to transform the economy, which was exactly what they wanted. In the early 1990s, China's central government resolved to establish carmaking as a so-called Pillar Industry, one that would—on its own—serve as a central support for dozens of others.

With this single decision to nurture the automotive industry and make private car ownership commonplace, China hoped to provide economic stimulus, create jobs, and boost growth in industries like steelmaking, glass, rubber, energy, and construction. These in turn were expected to stimulate higher demand for the extraction and processing of related commodities, such as iron ore, aluminum, cement, and more. On top of it all, there would emerge an entire automotive service sector ranging from gas stations, repair shops, and car washes to dealer and distribution networks, along with the car financing and insurance industries.

The logic seemed to make sense at the time, and it has largely panned out in the years since. China has already become the world's third largest car market, after the United States and Japan, and that has been achieved with relatively tiny penetration rates. By 2006, China had just eight passenger cars per thousand people. That compares with rates ranging from four hundred to six hundred per thousand among developed countries.

With numbers like that, it is not surprising that just about all of the world's major carmakers have already made their way into China, and some have laid down multibillion-dollar bets for their place at the table. The "must-be-in-China" logic is probably more compelling in this sector than any other.

As global majors have paired up in joint ventures with the biggest and the best of China's local producers, overall quality standards and competitiveness have gone up. Their higher demands have in turn forced improvements in the quality standards of Chinese parts producers—so much so that foreign firms that have thus far hesitated to source parts or components in China because of quality concerns should now reconsider.

Another direct result of increasing competitiveness is that China's highly fragmented car industry is facing sharp pressure to consolidate. At the end of 2005, China had 145 vehicle producers and more than forty-three hundred parts manufacturers. These were joined by nearly eighteen hundred more automotive enterprises engaged in activities such as engine production or vehicle refitting. Those numbers used to be even higher. In recent years, the least efficient and least viable firms have either failed or been gobbled up. A very high proportion of the remaining players still lack the scale, the capital, or the management and technical expertise they need to succeed, and no one doubts that coming years will see a dramatic further paring down of the number of firms.

Therefore a vital first step for any foreign player involved in any aspect of the automotive business in China is to cast a realistic and skeptical eye over all potential suppliers or partners. Simply put, do they have what it takes to survive the massive cull now under way in this industry? The right answer to that question up front can help you avert costly false starts and disruptions down the road.

One very predictable consequence of the vast overcrowding in the Chinese automotive sector has been lower prices and thinner margins. The undeniable long-term potential of this market means that all the foreign firms now piling in are probably right when they conclude that they need to be in China. But there is also an undeniable reality at this stage: Profits are not keeping pace with the skyrocketing sales numbers.

Passenger car sales in China in 2005 totaled nearly four million units, a 21.4 percent increase over the previous year. But with so much aggressive price cutting, that translated into just a 1 percent rise in sales revenue. Taken together, it added up to a 30 percent year-on-year decline in profits. (Motorcycle manufacturers, with a modest 5.5 percent increase, were the only segment of the industry to see any positive profit growth in 2005 at all.)

The message for foreign players in this field is clear: You may well need to be in China in these early stages to establish your presence, build market share, and simply avoid missing the boat; but you will need patience when it comes to seeing payouts. Most analysts are confident that overcapacity and downward price pressures will remain a part of the China car story for a long time yet to come.

Riding Shotgun in the Auto Sector

Chapter 4 will talk more about the peculiarities of marketing cars in China. But regardless of how the winners and losers shake out among the global majors now in the driver's seat, China's automotive sector is also generating plenty of opportunities for anyone willing to ride shotgun across a range of related products and services.

Demand for electronic navigational services, for example, has begun to take off. Satellite-based systems are already widely available and increasingly popular across China. So-called location-based system (LBS) services are also emerging, which use the ability of cell phone networks to pinpoint a driver's location and provide navigational support. Worth about $28 million in 2005, China's LBS market is expected to reach three hundred cities and mushroom to a value of $656 million by 2008.

Auto financing is another field with strong potential. Currently only about 10 percent of Chinese car buyers take out loans for their purchases. China will take a long time to reach the 70 percent level that is common in more developed markets, but there is no doubt it will be moving in that direction.

One reason for the difference is China's greater general aversion to consumer borrowing. Unlike the vast numbers of Americans who are perfectly comfortable with the "buy-now-pay-later" ethic, many Chinese remain reluctant to take on debt, especially for discretionary purchases. But this traditional attitude is already showing signs of changing.

Another factor has been China's poorly developed systems for tracking credit histories and evaluating risk or creditworthiness. Largely because of those shortcomings, the early entrants into Chinese car financing have not fared well. But those systems are now developing and, as they do, the volume and profitability of car financing can be expected to climb. While many major foreign carmakers have already been allowed to establish financing subsidiaries of their own, regulations for the most part restrict them to operating in a single location. The field therefore remains very much open.

Opportunities abound in still other related businesses. For example, China's State Environmental Protection Administration (SEPA) issued new regulations in 2006 mandating tough recycling and recovery standards for the end-of-life disposal of old cars. Material recovery rates that now stand at around 20 percent are to be lifted to 90 percent by 2017. China is likely to need a good deal of foreign technology and expertise before it gets anywhere close to that goal.

Then there are the less obvious opportunities. A great example of an American firm that found an imaginative, if roundabout, way to tap into China's burgeoning automotive sector is eChinaCash. Chaired by Peter Norton (of Norton anti-virus software fame), the company has partnered with Sinopec, China's largest gasoline retailer, to run a customer loyalty program based on a gas card.

The idea is simple enough. Customers prepay to store value on their cards, which they use to buy gas and earn award points across Sinopec's vast nationwide network of thirty thousand outlets. EChinaCash gets a tiny slice of each transaction. Sinopec, meanwhile, gets the benefit of streamlined management of its cash receipts and a valuable mechanism for generating customer loyalty.

But Norton, describing the venture in eChinaCash's sleekly furnished office in central Beijing, grew more animated as he came to the heart of the matter. "There's all that data," he said, "with its potential for data mining, and of understanding your customer better, servicing him better, marketing the right things to him, finding out who's buying what kind of gas, what kind of volumes. Are they moving around, very mobile? Or are they buying everything in the same neighborhood?"

Analyzing that data, eChinaCash works with Sinopec to build cross-brand and cross-sectoral marketing campaigns. In essence, it functions as Sinopec's internal marketing department. In Norton's mind, it all comes under the rubric of bringing Western expertise in "advanced consumer capitalism" to a huge Chinese enterprise that badly needs it, and doing it at just the right moment.

"Ten years ago, we'd be too early with this, and ten years from now everyone but the sleepiest Chinese company will be doing this, capturing lots of data and using it in a productive way," said Norton.

From the point of view of Sinopec, a vast old-style Chinese enterprise with a state-run pedigree, linking up with a new-economy partner such as eChinaCash was not an intuitive choice. But according to eChinaCash president and CEO Andrew Beck, that apparent mismatch was actually the key to making it happen, because it meant there was no chance eChinaCash would ever come after the oil company's core business. Instead of taking a piece of Sinopec's pie, eChina-Cash promised, it would be adding cream on top of it.

"It would have been very difficult for the Chinese government to allow Sinopec to partner with a large Western oil company," said Beck.

Good for What Ails You: The Biotech and Medical Sector

In the spring of 2003, much of China was turned upside down by the outbreak of severe acute respiratory syndrome (SARS). A mysterious and highly contagious pneumonia-like illness that first occurred in southern China and then spread around much of the world, SARS caused panic, economic disruption, and more than eight hundred deaths before it was finally brought under control.

Especially hard hit was the city of Beijing, which descended into a tense and eerie quiet. People retreated behind protective face masks and shunned public places, afraid of either catching the disease or simply getting caught on the wrong side of a quarantine barricade.

At the time, it was the Chinese government's botched handling of the epidemic that garnered much of the world's attention. By failing for months to disclose what was really going on, Chinese officials hampered efforts to slow the spread of the disease. They also badly damaged their own credibility in the eyes of their own people and the world.

Covered in greater detail in chapter 5, the transparency and credibility issues raised by the government's poor performance on SARS are vitally important. But by the time the dust had settled and the crisis had passed, another crucial issue had come clearly into view: China's health care system suffered from major shortcomings and needed help—including the kind of help that spells opportunity for foreign medical and biotech firms.

Of course, foreign business has been active in the sector

for years. (In fact, by way of full disclosure, I should mention here that Chindex International, a company co-founded by my wife, Roberta Lipson, was one of the earliest American entrants into this sector and remains a leading player, supplying imported medical equipment and operating joint-venture hospitals in China.)

Some of the very earliest and very largest foreign investments in China have been made by leading American or European pharmaceutical companies, and the sector has amply justified their optimism. Pharmaceutical sales in China by the top ten multinationals have been growing at an annual rate of about 15 percent since 1999. It is one of the sectors most directly threatened by the sort of rampant Chinese trademark and copyright violations covered in more detail in chapter 2. That threat notwithstanding, it is a market that is expected to grow to a value of $25 billion a year by 2010.

Meanwhile, the financially well-endowed elite hospitals in China's major cities have long been buying the latest and greatest in top-shelf imported equipment. Farther down the scale, hospital budgets are more constrained, and those in rural areas are often woefully short of even the most basic resources. But in Chinese cities, most hospitals manage to equip themselves adequately.

In fact, the health care shortcomings highlighted by the SARS drama have little to do with a lack of equipment or, for that matter, any deficiencies in the training or medical capabilities of Chinese doctors. The issues instead have to do with the nature of the system, along with poor management, efficiency, and service standards.

It is not hard to understand why the system developed the way it did. As a socialist country, China for decades provided health care as a basic social benefit, and while consumers spent little or nothing to get it, they could not choose where to go. They were tied to a designated provider, and as a result they had zero leverage.

Today most Chinese people can choose where to spend their health care dollars, and wherever they go they demand value and satisfaction in return—sometimes quite aggressively. In the past, when they were passive recipients of whatever health care was made available to them, consumers tended to take it for what it was and hope for the best outcome.

But now, after adjusting to the rude shock of having to pay for their own health care, their mood has changed dramatically. After spending their own money, rather than the state's, people want results. Many Chinese doctors have been physically attacked by patients and their families after bad outcomes. Patients can also be quick to sue or, just as menacing, threaten to publicize an allegation of malpractice. Anyone providing health care services in China needs to be well aware of this aggressive new tendency, and well prepared to respond.

These new and demanding consumer attitudes are already forcing improvements in the health care system—but government-run hospitals, for a variety of complex reasons, are finding reforms to be slow going. The persistently poor performance of China's health care system has been a major source of frustration to many Chinese. In a rare admission of a policy failure, the Chinese government itself acknowledged in 2005 that its efforts at reforming the system were simply not working. All this presents big opportunities for foreign firms equipped to deliver better results.

Chinese health care expenditures, rising 13 percent annually since 1990, still make up less than 5 percent of the nation's GDP. While there is no reason to think that figure should ever reach America's abnormally high level of 16 percent, there is no reason to doubt it will soon move closer to the 8 percent rate typical of other developed countries. Some analysts predict the size of China's health care industry will equal that of the United States by 2020. In 2005, China's imports of medical products amounted to almost $12 billion, an 18.5 percent rise from the previous year.

Not all of the opportunities for foreign firms are in selling. China can also be a potentially attractive location for biotech R&D operations, at least for companies that think carefully and realistically about their reasons for doing it.

China's regulatory environment offers one potential advantage, but Western companies need to tread especially carefully here. In China, things are far more lax when it comes to the rules governing clinical research. Patient consent requirements are less stringently enforced; animal research is more loosely regulated (and animal rights protests are virtually unknown); research involving stem cells, embryonic tissue, or the like isn't considered the least bit controversial. While most Western companies would be reluctant to do things in China that did not comply with standards at home, the fact remains that they do encounter fewer constraints there.

Lower cost is another obvious reason to consider putting biotech R&D in China. Lab facilities, scientific talent, and overhead can all be significantly cheaper. According to one industry survey, Chinese scientists repatriating after Western educations could be hired in China for 30 percent less than someone with a comparable education working in the West. Locally educated Chinese scientists could, of course, be hired for far less still.

But such savings can be easily offset by other factors, including the expense of importing sophisticated equipment or research supplies to China, or the cost of sending and keeping Western staff there. There are also intangible costs associated with the related bureaucratic requirements, and the natural friction of cross-cultural operations. If cost cutting alone is the objective, these offsets need to be anticipated and carefully weighed.

Quite apart from cost calculations, there are other potential drawbacks. In the late 1990s, I heard firsthand about the difficulties encountered by a senior executive who was sent to Beijing by one of the world's largest pharmaceutical companies to set up a research operation. What he found was sloppy science, messy academic politics, and endless frustration.

His Chinese researchers, he said, seemed less interested in truth or accuracy and more interested in returning what they thought were the desired results. If a compound was being tested for its ability to lower blood pressure, for example, his researchers would skew the results to show that it worked.

"They didn't seem to understand that it was just as valuable to us to establish that something *didn't* work. That's all part of the process of inquiry, but instead they just kept trying to give us positive results," he said.

The executive traced some of his other problems back to an earlier tactical mistake he'd made. Determined to spare no cost and do things right, he chose to collaborate with the top Chinese people in any given field, on the assumption that these department heads and senior researchers would be the most talented and accomplished around. Instead he found himself working with people who were more accomplished as politicians and bureaucratic infighters, and whose science skills were either rusty or lacking altogether.

Things have improved since then. Talking about his company's R&D experiences in China, Dan Vasella, CEO of Swiss pharmaceutical giant Novartis, was familiar with the very same pitfalls, but seemed to see them fading away in the rear-view mirror.

"The cost per individual researcher is lower here, but I'd look at the quality," Vasella told me in late 2004. "It doesn't help to have lots of cheap people if they are not doing any good work. That, however, is not the case here. The quality of people is constantly improving, and they now have some world-class people here. Because of the Cultural Revolution, there was something of a gap in the training, which affected the current generation of older senior people in the field."

But those people are now moving on, Vasella continued, and are being replaced by a younger generation that is very well trained, including many who have benefited from studying abroad. Novartis, he said, planned to quadruple its number of Chinese patient clinical trials within two years.

Quite apart from these improvements, there is another consideration—one that explains why the other executive, despite all the frustration he encountered, opted to keep his China R&D operation going. His company wasn't in it only for what the program could generate in the way of good science or cost savings, but rather as a way of bolstering its China presence for the long haul.

A recent study carried out by the Boston Consulting Group (BCG) advised other companies to consider that same compelling logic. "By investing more heavily and in more complex areas of R&D in China," BCG advised, "a multinational pharmaceutical company can signal its commitment to the Chinese market and strengthen relationships with key opinion leaders and officials there—thus increasing its chances of thriving in the health care market now taking shape in China."

Good Chemistry? The Chemical Sector

It should come as no surprise that China is looming large on the radar screens of the world's leading chemical firms. Domestic Chinese demand for their products is growing quickly, and at the same time many of the industry's biggest global customers—textile, car, and electronics makers—are moving more and more of their own operations to China. So whether it's for commodity chemicals or specialty chemicals, whether it's as inputs for domestic consumption or for export goods, China's hunger for chemicals is growing.

China's share of global chemical demand rose from 15 percent in 2004 to an estimated 20 percent in 2006. That can only go higher if, as some analysts predict, China's share of global factory output continues moving from its current level of around 8 percent to an expected level of 25 percent by 2025.

Most industries need to temper their China bullishness with that ever-important caveat—namely, that only a fraction of the nation's vast population so far has enough buying power to rate as potential customers. But when it comes to chemicals, the calculations are a little different. Chemicals are used in just about everything. So the end users who will be boosting demand are not limited to China's newly affluent buyers of cars and the latest luxury products.

According to Jörg Wuttke of the German chemical giant BASF, China is now entering a "sweet spot of demographic development" as ten to fifteen million people move each year from the countryside into cities all across China.

"These people are going from incomes of 100 euros per year to 100 euros per month, and this is a hell of a difference," said Wuttke, general manager for BASF China Company, Ltd. "Once they reach this level, they want different shoes, different wallpaper, and they want to start buying electronics."

This urbanization trend, Wuttke predicted, will kick-start chemical consumption over the next three to five years. "And it's not just the Beijings and the Shanghais of China, but it will be the places like Benxi, Anshan, and Dandong," he said, reeling off the names of second-tier Chinese cities that don't often get the attention of Western marketers.

Even in chemicals, however, not everything is sweetness and light. As in other sectors, sometimes the China market giveth, and sometimes it taketh away. Chinese chemical firms are steadily improving their quality and efficiency, and gaining the ability to compete effectively, especially in certain specialty chemicals. So in addition to fending off these potential competitors in global markets, foreign chemical firms are facing another significant challenge. Many of their best international customers, having moved production facilities to China, will increasingly be tempted to source their chemicals from local competitors.

The sector also faces the looming threat of overcapacity and declining margins—"in China everybody and his grandmother is apparently building a chemical plant," Wuttke said. Indeed, like the auto industry, China's domestic chemical industry is highly fragmented, with many small and inefficient producers getting weeded out all the time.

A special concern for the chemical industry is of course safety, and in China the picture isn't always pretty. For decades, safety and environmental considerations have taken a backseat to the imperatives of growth and production. A chemical spill in the Songhua River made headlines in 2005 when it poisoned the water supply for millions of residents downstream, including some across the border in Russia.

Taking the helm after that episode, a new environment minister, Zhou Shengxian, warned that one hundred Chinese chemical plants constituted safety hazards. For too long, Zhou said, China's approach was "pollution and destruction first, regulations later."

Western firms in this sector need to be extremely cautious about any potential liabilities connected with any local firms they partner with. On the positive side, foreign companies are far more experienced and far better positioned than Chinese competitors to comply with stricter environmental regulations. For their part, Chinese firms will soon be getting away with a lot less corner cutting than they are used to.

Building for Success: The Construction and Infrastructure Sector

Walking through Beijing's central business district from one meeting to another on a wintry day in 2005, it occurred to me that this is what it must have felt like to walk the streets of New York in the 1930s. My short trip was an obstacle course of makeshift walkways between building sites. Construction noise was coming from everywhere—above, below, and all around. Some of the projects were huge, hulking buildings nearly finished. Others were still just holes in the ground, cavernous foundations waiting to be poured. Here in Beijing, I thought, I was glimpsing a work in progress that, like New York seventy years earlier, would really be something amazing once it was finished—assuming, of course, that the whole city didn't simply sink under the sheer mass of all that concrete, steel, and glass being welded together and stacked up in one place.

And it's not just Beijing. From the dust that fills the air to the cranes that dot the skylines of so many Chinese cities, the evidence of China's construction boom is everywhere. Apartment buildings. Hotels. Office towers and shopping centers. Airports, factories, and power plants. The list goes on and on.

As one Bush administration official recently put it during testimony before a congressional committee, China has been constructing 4.3 billion square feet of building space—the rough equivalent of a thousand Sears Towers—every year for the past fifteen years. According to a World Bank estimate, China will account for the construction of half the world's new buildings between now and 2015.

Nationwide, the investment in construction and installation in 2004 totaled $517 billion. Of course, not all of that business is up for grabs for foreign firms—far from it. A 2001 report by Hong Kong's Trade and Development Council estimated that 15 percent of the sector was then accessible to foreign participation.

Even at that level, though, the available piece of the pie in 2004 would have been worth more than $77 billion. But since joining the WTO at the end of 2001, market access for foreigners has improved significantly. Meanwhile the pie itself has continued to grow: The 2004 investment figures marked an increase of 208 percent from four years earlier.

As they compete for this business with domestic contractors and equipment suppliers, foreign firms face some serious disadvantages. Not least, they are poorly positioned to match the personal and professional connections that local firms have with the municipal government officials who control so much of China's building expenditures. Indeed, many Chinese construction firms operate directly under city governments.

Foreign firms are also handicapped by the onerous requirements they need to meet to qualify for projects above a certain size. They must commit significant sums of registered capital and maintain prohibitively high staffing levels.

But they also have advantages. For one thing, many high-value projects are commissioned by China-based subsidiaries of multinational corporations that need to meet home-country quality standards. These MNCs may have doubts about the ability of local contractors to deliver at that level. They may also prefer to work with Western companies that they have previously dealt with in other markets.

With their broader range of services, foreign building companies have another potential advantage: Domestic Chinese firms tend to be highly specialized. Some provide design and engineering services, others handle procurement, and still others do project management and actual construction work. Diversified foreign building companies thus have a distinct edge with potential clients who are seeking a more integrated approach to a building project.

Foreign companies are better able to meet China's increasingly strict environmental standards as well. At both the national and local levels, the Chinese government is promoting badly needed "Green Building" initiatives, and Chinese companies in general are far behind in their ability to supply the right equipment, materials, and expertise. Firms such as Carrier, Honeywell, Siemens, and General Electric are already on the ground, providing energy-efficient and water-saving technologies, and there is plenty of room for more.

Much has been made of the potential connected to the 2008 Beijing Olympic Games. While significant marketing and service-sector opportunities do exist, the window for getting in is closing fast as the games draw near, and when it comes to the Olympic building spree, it is clearly too late already. But the timing is far better for a similar boom now under way in Shanghai, which is preparing to host the World Expo in 2010. The city expects to welcome seventy million visitors between May and October of that year, and it is determined to dazzle them with its new architecture.

Apart from all the gleaming buildings themselves, China is also spending billions on its transport infrastructure. If Beijing is reminiscent of New York in the 1930s, then China's current road-building endeavor can only be compared to America's construction of the interstate highway system in the 1950s.

As another by-product of the automotive Pillar Industry strategy, the country has been building roads at an astonishing rate. From 2000 to 2004, China doubled the length of its top-grade highways to twenty-one thousand miles, and current plans call for doubling that again by 2020. Some experts doubt even that will be enough to satisfy growing road freight demands.

With most of China's major cities already linked by major highways, the government is now working to extend the asphalt lifeline to an additional 750 million rural residents. In both the countryside within an hour of Beijing and the far-off hills of southwestern Yunnan Province, I have visited towns that were utterly transformed once they got connected to the road grid. By linking more such areas to the rest of China and the world beyond, this initiative will, over the longer term, have a huge wealth-generating impact on local economies throughout the country.

In the shorter term, it will bring huge opportunities to foreign equipment suppliers. Morgan Stanley expects the government to spend $148 billion between 2006 and 2010 on this road-building effort, with much of the money going to building materials suppliers and construction contractors.

With China's trade volume growing so rapidly, it is hardly surprising that its ports and railways also continue to absorb investment. Chinese ports, which have long been receptive to foreign involvement, continue to expand, and continue to achieve impressive standards of efficiency.

Railways, by contrast, have been notoriously closed to foreign participation. The rail system has also received less money from the government; highways in 2004 received more than five times as much. Not coincidentally, the railways have performed poorly, failing to keep up with rising freight demands and causing frequent delivery bottlenecks.

Encouraged by the way foreign involvement has helped boost the road and port sectors, the government made tentative moves in late 2005 toward opening up the rail sector as well. For the period 2006–2010, it budgeted about six thousand miles of new track, more than doubling the average annual building pace of the previous ten years.

In nontransport infrastructure, water projects—on both the treatment and the supply sides—are another huge opportunity. Never well endowed with water resources to begin with, China has been straining for years under severe shortages, especially in the northern part of the country.

A big part of the problem has been China's water pricing policies. Until the late 1980s, no one paid anything at all for water, and as a result no one had any incentive to conserve it. While it hesitates to stress farmers and industries by raising fees too rapidly, the government has already begun to price this scare resource more rationally, making investments in this sector more economically feasible all the time.

Rising Power, Bright Prospects: The Energy Sector

Over the past ten years, the Chinese government has had an awful time trying to gauge the nation's power needs, and it has caused some serious problems by getting things wrong. Granted, it is a complicated task anywhere, and one that has occasionally been mismanaged even in the United States, where markets are mature, growth is modest and largely predictable, and demand fluctuations are mostly attributable to weather variations.

But consider all the additional variables at work in China. Economic growth has for years been at or above double digits. Pricing and regulatory policies are being overhauled constantly; and whole new industries are springing up in all corners of the country. Consumption patterns are in flux, and massive internal migrations see tens of millions of laborers on the move. All this makes it pretty tough for Chinese planners to predict how much power will be needed and where.

Foreign players in the power sector face a similar dilemma, and—given the high cost of investing in new refining facilities, generating capacity, or transmission networks—they likewise face severe risks. But with so much potential upside, these are risks they are clearly prepared to tolerate. From Saudi oil giant Aramco to ExxonMobil, foreign firms have already invested billions of dollars in China.

Just how much energy will China need? Government planners counted on annual power demand increases of around 5 percent for each year between 2001 and 2005, and when actual demand for each of those years rose twice as fast, power providers were caught short. All across China, cities were plagued by electricity shortages, with frequent supply cuts to homes and factories alike. Indeed, many factories in China have had to invest in their own diesel-powered generating systems to protect themselves against intermittent outages.

Following a splurge of new capacity built in the last few years, China has just about managed to alleviate most of the shortages. With still more capacity in the works, it has also sparked some concerns about a potential glut. But the far greater likelihood is rapid and sustained demand growth, bringing with it huge and varied opportunities all across the energy sector.

Per capita, China now consumes only about one-seventh as much electricity as the United States. But while the American number hardly changes, China's is shooting up fast. That same "sweet spot of demographic development" that Jörg Wuttke of BASF believes will boost chemical sales is likely to boost electricity consumption at the same time. For many of the ten to fifteen million people he spoke of who are relocating each year from the countryside to China's cities, the move will mean owning a refrigerator for the first time. Following on closely will be appliances of all types, with power-hungry air conditioners near the top of the list.

What's more, new power demand will not come solely from those who are newly able to afford their appliances. There is also demand that has built up during the recent years of short electricity supply. Plenty of people who have long had the money and the desire to buy air conditioners will only really do so once they are confident of getting the power they'll need to run them.

There are still thirty million people in China who lack access to electricity, but most of them will be getting it soon. By 2010, China plans to invest about $75 billion in new generating plants, and another $100 billion on expansion and upgrades of the transmission grid.

Mainly because of government-mandated price controls, foreign firms have had trouble making money by producing power in China, and most have given up. But with all this planned spending, prospects are bright for business in engineering services and equipment sales.

Relying as it does on its own abundant coal resources for about two-thirds of its power generation, China is especially eager to absorb clean-coal technology from foreign suppliers. This is clearly an area with some of the greatest long-term potential for foreign companies, especially since most experts expect coal to dominate China's energy mix for the next twenty-five years.

Though many Western skeptics doubt it can meet its goals, China has vowed to boost renewables to 15 percent of its total energy mix by 2020. If it does fail, it won't be for lack of trying. The government is committing $184 billion to the cause, and it knows that much of this will be going to foreign firms.

While foreign companies now play a huge role in China's energy sector, it was not always thus. Twenty years ago, an energy-self-sufficient China was a net exporter of both coal and crude oil, and apart from some imported turbines it had very little Western involvement in the sector.

In 1993, China became a net importer of oil, and by 2003 its daily oil consumption had climbed to six and a half million barrels per day, catapulting it past Japan as the world's second largest consumer after the United States.

As yet another consequence of the automotive Pillar Industry strategy, China's oil demand, together with its dependency on imports, is growing year by year. Analysts from the US Department of Energy and the International Energy Agency agree that Chinese oil consumption is likely to double to about twelve million barrels a day by 2025, and that it will need to import about three-quarters of that amount.

A latecomer to the oil import game, China has had to scramble to find suppliers with spare output that is not already committed to the United States, Europe, or Japan. But China does have one advantage here: Unlike so many Western countries, where policy considerations and public opinion hinder cooperation with some of the world's more unsavory regimes, China has no such qualms. Throughout Africa and Central Asia, China has been more than happy to ignore politics and focus instead on energy deals with the likes of Angola, Sudan, Iran, and Uzbekistan.

With all that new oil coming in, China is also scrambling to develop enough refining capacity. In terms of both technology and management, most existing Chinese refineries lag behind world standards, making this another area where it is looking for foreign help.

Regulations prohibit foreign investors from taking majority holdings in any Chinese refineries, and even any minority stakes require burdensome approval procedures. Acknowledging the need for more foreign expertise, however, Chinese officials speak frequently of easing these restrictions. But that may prove difficult, since the energy sector is managed by an interagency jumble of regulators that is, even for China, unusually cumbersome.

In addition to the State Electricity Regulatory Commission and the National Development and Reform Commission, which have the most direct control, there are half a dozen other departments with formal roles of their own. Among others, these include the Ministries of Finance, Commerce, and Foreign Affairs. The involvement of provincial and local governments only adds to the complexity.

A large part of what all these bureaucrats concern themselves with is pricing policy. They want to avoid inflation and the related social instability it could cause. They also want to avoid stressing some of the larger state-owned enterprises that employ millions but can barely keep themselves afloat. So at every point along the way, from coal producers to power plants to grid operators, state-mandated price controls limit what they can charge.

As with water, the government knows that price caps are holding the industry back, and, to the great relief of both foreign and domestic energy companies, it is moving slowly toward more rational levels.

Money in the Bank: The Finance Sector

When the renowned American renegade Willie Sutton was asked by a priest why he robbed banks, he answered with the immortal words, "Because that's where the money is." It is the same simple logic that has foreign investors eyeing business with Chinese banks and other financial institutions. That is undoubtedly "where the money is," but for the longest time, getting at it proved about as challenging and as risky in China as it was for Willy Sutton in the middle of the last century.

Since joining the World Trade Organization, China has undertaken firm commitments to let foreign banks, insurance companies, and brokers tap the local market. But the financial sector was one that the Chinese government was all along most worried about exposing to foreign competition, and it has seen some of the worst foot dragging. The scene has been dominated by investment caps, lending limits, and geographic or category restrictions, and foreign bankers seem to devote as much time and effort to pursuing approvals as they do looking for business.

But restrictions are now being lifted, and foreign banks are allowed to do more varied kinds of business, including credit card business and local currency transactions with Chinese enterprises. They are also playing a huge (and often lucrative) role in the restructuring and listing of Chinese banks.

As more restrictions peel away, foreign banks will eventually be allowed to handle local currency deposits from individual depositors. As their scope and success expand, however, the local banking industry complains more loudly about its vulnerability.

Those complaints are apparently being heeded. In remarks that struck considerable fear into the hearts of foreign bankers in China in 2005, Shi Jiliang, vice chairman of the China Banking Regulatory Commission, noted that foreign banks were growing faster than anticipated. "We need to think about having an appropriate level of protection for Chinese banks," he told an industry forum.

Shi spoke of staying within the bounds of China's WTO commitments while at the same time "containing the pace and geographic extension of foreign banks' market entry so as to leave some time and space for Chinese banks to embrace the full-scale competition." It is hard to see how those two could be reconciled, and the CBRC later explained that Shi was merely giving his personal opinion.

As with so much else in China, the opening of the banking sector is a mixed picture. True, Shi may have hinted ominously at more restrictions, but local regulators in Beijing have actually permitted foreign banks to apply for and receive RMB licenses a full year ahead of the WTO-mandated timetable. Overall the trend is moving the right way: Foreign banks will find more to do in China, and more ways to do it.

The concerns of domestic banks are understandable, but many Western bankers believe Chinese banks have less to fear than they seem to think. Domestic banks have massive national coverage, with local branches in thousands of small towns across the country. While there are valid fears that large foreign banks might siphon off higher-value customers, they seem unlikely to ever replicate the coverage or name recognition of their local competitors.

Beyond the issue of gaining approvals for their business, foreign bankers must also grapple with China's poor protection of creditors' rights. Combined with the country's equally underdeveloped system of credit history reporting, it is a potentially dangerous combination. For decades, Chinese banks functioned less as commercial lenders and more as government allocation agencies. State-owned enterprises, many of them dreadfully inefficient and chronically unprofitable, were funded by state-mandated bank loans. Creditworthiness was not an issue, and loan foreclosure was not an option.

Now Chinese banking is moving closer to commercial terms, but the tools are still missing. Credit rating agencies are emerging and will surely develop over time. In the interim, though, a lot of bankers are flying blind as they seek to evaluate the worthiness of their would-be borrowers.

The protection of creditor rights may take even longer to improve. This may be the one area where China's market reforms collide most starkly with its desire to remain nominally socialist on some level. There is still a school of thought within China saying that if socialism is to mean anything at all, it must at least mean this: A bank run by wealthy capitalists should not be able to throw defaulting borrowers out of their home or business.

The impulse may be noble, but it leads to obvious problems. As a 2005 report by the American Chamber of Commerce in China (AmCham) put it, "years of waiting have still not yielded a law that gives creditors the right they need to impose market discipline on borrowers.... The system currently provides excessive protection to borrowers and leads to an abnormally high level of non-performing loans." The lack of adequate legal infrastructure in the banking field, the report added, "presents a significant, and potentially unacceptable risk to all banks."

Other aspects of the Chinese finance sector are plagued by equally onerous problems. Both capital markets and the insurance sector remain highly regulated and grossly inefficient. In 2006, Chinese stock markets finally began a solid resurgence, but that followed a prolonged four-year slump. Indeed, according to Shan Weijian, managing partner of Newbridge Capital and one of China's shrewdest financiers, Chinese stock markets are not performing the role they should. "Stock markets are not an engine of growth. In fact they are a drag on the economy," he said in 2006 in the *China Economic Review.*

They have also been a drag on the personal finances of many. A 2006 survey by the *China Securities Journal* found that 77 percent of all Chinese stock investors had lost money over the previous year. The reasons are not hard to understand. With poor standards of corporate governance, accounting, and financial disclosures, the stock markets are virtually a casino. After four down years starting in 2001, Chinese stock markets enjoyed a solid upturn in 2006, but there remains precious little correlation between the fundamentals and the share price performance of listed Chinese companies.

The problem is exacerbated by the rampant trading of inside information. Indeed, the position of outside investors is akin to that of a gambler betting at a track where the races are fixed. They lack the necessary, most basic decision-making tools, but the betting window is open and even if they don't have an inside line on the fix, they stand a chance of getting lucky and picking a winner anyway.

The vast prospects of the Chinese insurance sector, meanwhile, have attracted tremendous foreign interest as well as significant frustration. Between 1996 and 2002, according to the Boston Consulting Group, insurance premium income in China grew 40 percent annually. Continued growth rates as high as 25 percent were predicted for the foreseeable future, with the sector's market value reaching more than $100 billion by 2008.

There is no mystery as to why China's insurance sector looks so promising. State-managed health insurance is giving way to commercial insurance, and the state pension system is falling apart at a time when demographic trends point to a rapidly aging population.

But the market suffers from a lack of good actuarial data, and also from poorly designed insurance products. Chinese companies have yet to learn what they need to know about developing more sophisticated offerings and selling them effectively. The Chinese public, meanwhile, remains poorly educated about its options. Foreign companies will have a major role to play in these areas.

Two last sectors—information technology/telecoms, and media and entertainment—also bear mentioning here. As huge sectors that are closely tied to multiple aspects of the China business scene, they are covered in some depth elsewhere in this book in ways that will leave you with a clear sense of their impact, and of the unique challenges facing foreign firms. Suffice it to say at this point that foreign companies will have a huge role to play—both in the accelerating drive to capture, inform, and entertain China's 2.6 billion eyeballs, and the building and running of the high-tech infrastructure that will be needed to do it.

KEY POINTS TO REMEMBER
FROM CHAPTER 1

1. The Chinese automotive sector is in the midst of a profound consolidation, so regardless of what you are preparing to do, a vital first step is to objectively evaluate all potential local partners or suppliers. How likely are they to survive the massive cull now under way?

2. Over decades of having their health care choices made for them, Chinese consumers were resigned to mediocre service. But now that they have gained a say in where they spend their health care dollars, they demand value and satisfaction in return—sometimes quite aggressively. Violent attacks on physicians and malpractice suits have both become commonplace.

3. Restrictions on biotech research are far looser in China than most Western countries. Animal rights are barely an issue. There is little controversy over

research involving stem cells or embryonic tissue, and patient consent requirements are loose. Any Western company hoping to comply with its home-country standards, rather than China's, will need to keep on top of local staff at all times in order to know what exactly is going on—and making sure no one crosses the line.

4. China's chemical industry, like the auto industry, is highly fragmented; smaller, less efficient producers are getting weeded out all the time. Make sure you partner with players who will be there for the long haul.

5. In China's construction industry, domestic firms tend to be highly specialized, focusing either on design, procurement and project management, or actual construction. Diversified Western firms that are capable of handling all these elements can offer a fully integrated package and thus enjoy a distinct edge.

6. China's energy sector has huge upside potential, but it is governed by a matrix of competing agencies and ministries that is unusually cumbersome, even by Chinese standards. It also has exceptionally restrictive policies for foreign investors. Chinese officials have acknowledged the need to ease restrictions and streamline the regulatory tangle, but it will be a long time before they manage to actually do it. So if you are working in this sector, you need to be prepared for an extra-large helping of red tape.

7. The finance sector remains heavily restricted to foreign investors, who continue to struggle, almost deal

by deal, for the necessary approvals. Once they do get approvals to compete evenly with Chinese competitors, foreign bankers will nevertheless have problems matching their nationwide coverage. But lucrative deals are already happening as foreign investment banks participate in the restructuring and listing of Chinese banks. China's stock markets and insurance industry remain poorly developed and heavily regulated, and it will take a long time before their potential can be tapped.

2

Laws, Rules, and Regulations

When it comes to the law—the way laws are made, enforced, obeyed, and perceived—China presents something of a split personality.

On the one hand, the country has its reputation (often well earned) as a police state—a rigid authoritarian system in which today's Communist party leaders have merely replaced the emperors of old, ruling just as they did: by heavy-handed fiat. Forced to live under an inflexible one-party system, ordinary people have no voice, no choice, and no legal recourse.

But if there is any truth to that—and clearly there is some—why does China so often feel as lawless as the Wild West? How, in any kind of police state, can the law be so brazenly flouted so much of the time? From the simplest things, like basic traffic laws, to the most complex, such as the Byzantine regulations governing business operations, people in China very often do exactly what they want, instead of what the law would have them do.

For sociologists, political scientists, and legal scholars, this paradox provides a rich vein of academic inquiry, offering up boundless fodder for research and in-depth study.

For foreign business people, it is nothing short of a minefield.

Of course, a book like this could not possibly promise to guide you safely through it all. No book could. Like just about everything else in China, the legal system is complicated to begin with and evolving all the time. The pace of change is far too fast, and the variability across locales, industries, and circumstances is far too wild, for any book to tell you everything you need to know in any given situation. The only reliable universal advice is this: No matter what it is you are trying to do in China, you will need specialized, professional legal help on an ongoing basis.

This chapter will help familiarize you with China's legal system, describe the many vagaries that plague it, and walk you through the basics of the real-world issues you can expect to face.

What choices do foreign businesses have when it comes to structuring their China operations? How can they protect themselves against China's relentless copyright pirates? How can disputes be resolved? What about corruption, tax laws, and liability issues? The more background knowledge you have about these issues, the better equipped you will be to work with your legal professionals on the details.

But before delving into these and other areas, it will be useful to first take a quick big-picture look at how China's legal system works, and also how—very often—it doesn't.

FEW LAWYERS, AND FEW LAWYER JOKES

Keenly aware of how excessively litigious their own society is, Americans living and working in China tend to notice pretty quickly that lawyers have a much smaller role in Chinese society and the day-to-day workings of Chinese business.

And notwithstanding their general disdain for lawyers (and their love of a good lawyer joke), most of these Americans are equally quick to appreciate that China's relative dearth of lawyers is a serious problem. Or perhaps more accurately, it is a symptom of a serious problem, namely, the capricious and underdeveloped state of the legal system.

China now has about one lawyer for every thirteen thousand people, compared with one for every three hundred in the United States. Though seemingly low, that ratio actually marks a sharp rise over the past twenty-five years. In the heyday of Chairman Mao's rule, the courts were virtually sidelined. Law did not make for a very promising career choice.

In the words of Stanford University Professor Stanley Lubman, one of the leading Western experts on Chinese law, China's legal institutions and rules had by 1979 become "like crude buildings gone to ruin, but for which the architectural plans still remained."

Since then, China's ambitious legal reform efforts have largely focused on reviving and remodeling those institutions, and transforming the country's traditional system of "rule of man" into one of "rule of law."

Believe it or not, legal reform is a hot topic of conversation in Chinese business circles. You are not likely to be in China for long before you find yourself in an earnest discussion with local counterparts about the legal system, and very early in that discussion you are bound to hear the *rule of law* catchphrase.

But in both the academic literature and the popular press, Chinese commentators dance on the head of a pin about just what the term means. The Chinese phrase *yi fa zhi guo* is somewhat ambiguous, translatable into English as either "rule of law" or "rule by law." And the difference is actually very significant.

Rule of law implies that the law itself is in command, an independent and objective framework that can resist political interference, protect the rights of individuals, and constrain even the state or Communist party where necessary.

Rule by law suggests something else entirely: that instead of being a supreme and objective standard in its own right, the law is an instrument to be wielded by the party and the government in the exercise and preservation of their authority.

In actual practice, it is the rule-by-law model that still holds sway, and copious official rhetoric notwithstanding, there is little sign that the government intends to truly surrender its control of this powerful instrument and allow it to ever be used against its own interests.

To be fair, the government is doing more than just paying lip service to the rule-of-law concept. In many areas, it is genuinely working to introduce reforms to make China's system more rational and rule-governed. These changes are not only required under China's WTO-related commitments but will, the government knows, also benefit China by increasing the competitiveness of its economy and improving the overall efficiency of its business environment.

Because of this effort, the pace of change in the Chinese legal system is simply mind-boggling. Lawyers in China have to spend so much time keeping up with the flood of revisions and new laws announced by the government that it's a wonder they have any time left over to spend with clients. Take as a sample the month of October 2005. During that single month, China amended its Securities Law, changing the terms of public offerings, revising the rules of corporate takeovers, and modifying the rules governing the operation of securities firms.

In the same month, the China Insurance Regulatory Commission released new provisions that broadly shifted the terms by which insurance and reinsurance companies may structure their business, and it allowed the introduction of entirely new financial instruments and insurance products. And China introduced changes in its Company Law, its foreign exchange rules for multinational companies, and its taxation policies.

That month was by no means unusual. Laws and regulations are in constant flux in China. The rule changes come fast and furiously, affecting things like accounting, banking, and media one month; advertising, stock markets, retail sales, or property transactions the next.

The bad news about this is that you need to spend a lot of time, and pay for a lot of legal help, just to keep pace with it all and know where you stand. But the good news is that most of these changes are moving things in the right direction: toward greater clarity, greater consistency, and greater compatibility with international standards.

Yet in its own effort to dance on the head of that same theoretical pin, the government wants to gain all these benefits by increasing the role of the courts and the law, but without totally setting them free. It is this attempt to have it both ways that explains the split personality of China's legal system. Think of it as a Dr. Jekyll and Mr. Hyde story with Chinese characteristics.

MEET DR. JEKYLL...

As reforms advance, the legal system is growing not only more rational but also undeniably more responsive. Chinese citizens and foreign companies alike are increasingly able to access the courts to try to solve their problems. This access can be spotty, and so can the results, especially when it comes to the enforcement of verdicts, as you will soon discover in the examples provided later in this chapter. But as gaps in the code get filled in, and as lawyers and judges become more experienced and professional, things are clearly improving.

The government has also become more receptive to input as it makes new rules and modifies the old ones. This applies not only to the legislature's work in making actual laws, but also to the ministries and other executive departments responsible for drafting guidelines and regulations in areas ranging from taxation policy and investment approval to currency exchange procedures and product safety guidelines.

In a new and growing trend, the government is beginning to hold formal open hearings in which citizens, experts, and industry groups are allowed to at least offer input on proposed changes. Increasingly, even foreign business associations are given opportunities to offer input.

The American Chamber of Commerce in China is among the most active of all the foreign chambers, and it runs specialized industry committees that are in frequent contact with Chinese regulators. The input of these committees may not always be heeded, but it is certainly heard.

Feedback is also incorporated into decision making in other, less formal ways. One simple but illustrative example of this involves traffic rules. Not far from my own home in northeastern Beijing is a particularly messy five-way intersection. As the volume of city traffic has exploded in recent years, the police have experimented endlessly, groping for ways to unsnarl it. At various points, they have redrawn the turn lanes and reconfigured the traffic lights in different combinations. They tried prohibiting left turns from one side, to no avail. So they switched that back and prohibited left turns from the other side. Later they turned one of the roads into a one-way street.

But regardless of the constant changes, drivers more or less went where they wanted to anyway—unless, of course, barriers were put in place to physically block them, or traffic police stood in the intersection and actually enforced the new rules. With officers on the spot, drivers would suddenly start to obey—and the traffic would grow even more congested than usual.

After a while, the police ended up shaping the rules at this intersection around the actual traffic flow, and the results have been fairly good. Rush hour is still rush hour, but for the rest of the day the spot is no longer the chronic and acute bottle-neck it used to be.

Similar things happen all the time on a larger scale. Rules and laws are often ignored. The authorities tacitly acknowl-edge this every time they issue and then reissue (and sometimes re-reissue) their notices and "urgent circulars" emphasizing the importance of some law or regulation that nobody seems to be following. Sometimes the rules are enforced in short-lived periodic crackdowns—the equivalent of stationing traf-fic cops for a day in that five-way intersection. And many times, when a new rule doesn't take hold, the authorities sim-ply change it again.

Or they can ignore it. With so much discretionary power still in the hands of officials, many technicalities can be readily smoothed over, and creative paths can be navigated around would-be legal obstacles. Of course, it can cut either way, depending on whether those officials are well disposed toward you or toward your competitor.

There are obviously plenty of laws and regulations that are not open to such flexible interpretation or modification. But the fact that so many are, coupled with the arbitrary and often spotty enforcement of the rest, can quickly leave you with the feeling that the putative iron-fisted rulers of this "police state" are really not such tough guys after all.

...BUT REMEMBER MR. HYDE

It may come as a pleasant surprise for you to learn that the Chinese legal system, with its subtle flexibility and increasing responsiveness, has a kinder and gentler Dr. Jekyll side to it. But remember this: It would be a mistake all the same to turn your back on the system's Mr. Hyde.

While lax enforcement of the law means that thousands get away with corruption, fraud, tax evasion, and more, those who get caught are often treated harshly. The criminal justice system is structured such that any defendant who reaches court faces an almost insurmountable presumption of guilt. Acquittals are rare, and penalties are often harsh.

The death penalty is widely used. China does not publish figures, but international human rights groups believe that between five and ten thousand executions are carried out nationwide each year. And it is not just applied to murderers. Above a certain monetary threshold, so-called economic crimes can also be considered capital crimes. People have been executed in China for taking bribes, and even for falsifying tax receipts. In early 2006, Guangzhou, one of China's largest and most open cities, announced that even purse snatchers could be subject to the death penalty.

So the state and party have their stern side, and, wielding the law as one of their primary instruments of political control, they have yet to allow any part of the legal system to operate independently. That includes the legislature.

The National People's Congress (NPC) is nominally an elected representative legislative body, but in reality it is no such thing. It does have a permanent staff of legal experts who work yearlong to draft legislation, and those staffers are becoming increasingly professional. As a proper legislature, though, the NPC still operates very much as a showcase and a rubber stamp.

With nearly three thousand delegates, it meets in full session only once a year and with a great deal of pomp and pageantry. But it has never actually voted down a measure that was teed up for it by the central Communist party leadership. Between annual full sessions, held each year in March, a select group known as the NPC Standing Committee quietly handles the nation's lawmaking duties.

The rest of the legal system is likewise under the firm control of the party, which assigns political officers to the staff of every police department, law court, and prosecutor's office in the country.

On paper, China's constitution guarantees its citizens an impressive set of rights and protections, but in practice these can always be trumped by the whim of the party. That same flexibility that can be so pleasing when it gently allows things to go your way can be downright brutal when it swings against you.

The party's political commissars do not necessarily intervene in every case. But the fact remains that they always have the ability to do so, with no external checks or balances.

Lacking such checks, officials all too often resort to arbitrary enforcement of whatever rules they choose.

Often they use this power to act in the public interest (as they see it, anyway). But in far too many cases, they abuse these powers out of sheer self-interest. And as you do business in China, it is important to remember that while foreigners are generally treated with a lighter touch, they are *not* entirely immune to such behavior.

FROM THEORY TO PRACTICE

There is no doubt that the more background knowledge you gain about China's legal system, the easier you will find it to follow what's going on around you, and to understand what's going through the minds of the Chinese people you deal with. But what about the practical legal issues involved in doing business in China?

At the very top of the list is the question of how to structure a venture. Whether it's a manufacturing operation for exporting your products, a business aimed at selling in China, or a sourcing operation, your first crucial decision will be how to set it up.

Restrictions are easing all the time, and new, more flexible options are likely to appear in coming years. But for now, the main choices come down to joint ventures (either cooperative or equity); representative offices; and wholly foreign-owned enterprises.

Each has its own advantages and disadvantages, and not all of these options are available yet in all industries. In certain strategic sectors, such as telecom services, the government still limits the ability of foreigners to hold equity, making cooperative joint ventures the only possible option.

Where you do have a choice, you will need to consider a variety of trade-offs involving your level of control over the business, your tax status, your ability to invoice for goods and services within China, and your ability to move profits out.

JOINT VENTURES

In the earliest days of China's opening to Western business, there was really only one choice: the joint venture, or JV. And to this day, it is a term that strikes fear and contempt into the hearts of many foreign investors in China. A lot of the very worst China business horror stories you'll hear or read involve joint ventures gone horrendously wrong, and one of the earliest pieces of facile conventional wisdom you are likely to hear is that you should avoid joint ventures at all costs.

Like so much conventional wisdom, though, this advice oversimplifies things. To be sure, there are many risks and disadvantages with the joint-venture structure, and many dramatic and well-publicized failures have in fact been joint ventures. But it would be unfair to lay the blame for those failures entirely on the JV structure itself. Even today, despite the existence of other options, there are situations where JVs can make sense.

Some of the problems that plagued early JVs had less to do with the structure itself and more to do with the simple fact

that Chinese and foreign business people were equally unac-
customed to dealing with each other. These deals were like
arranged marriages between partners who, both metaphori-
cally and literally, did not speak the same language. On both
sides, they did not—indeed could not—understand where their
partners were coming from or hoped to go. Regardless of the
structure, unrealistic expectations and poor communication
were bound to cause problems.

Distortions in the Chinese regulatory environment also hin-
dered successful JV matchmaking in the early days. Throughout the 1980s, for example, the Chinese government sought
to encourage foreign investment by granting tax holidays and
import duty exemptions to joint ventures. For Chinese enterprises, the ability to import cars and other capital equipment
duty-free was incentive enough to start up a joint venture and
then do the bare minimum to just keep it breathing.

For a foreign partner who hoped to see that same venture
actually grow and make money, and who naively assumed the
Chinese partner shared the same basic goals, disappointment
was inevitable. As tax and customs regulations have grown
more rational, the potential for such grossly mismatched JV
expectations has diminished.

But hazards do remain. For instance, if there is political
involvement from local authorities, there is still a good chance
that your Chinese partner will be more interested in seeing a
venture generate jobs and tax revenue for the local economy
than profits to share with you. While this may be a somewhat
more laudable goal than scoring duty-free car imports, it will
hardly make for success on your end of the deal.

And if your local partners are simply unscrupulous, there is no shortage of ways they can find to exploit the structure for their own gain at the expense of the joint venture. In many cases, local partners have in effect subsidized other enterprises they owned by sourcing supplies or services at low cost from the joint venture.

Local JV partners have also been known to run overtime production in joint-venture factories, often using the foreign partner's proprietary designs or technology, and then dumping the output into domestic markets to compete directly against the products of the joint venture. In the most blatant cases, they simply shifted cash or other assets illicitly from the joint venture to another enterprise under its control.

In one case, which had already been dragging on for more than a decade when I began reporting on it in 2003, a group of investors from the United States, Canada, and Australia struggled endlessly to recoup the $4 million they'd sunk into a joint-venture hotel in the northeastern city of Dandong. Originally from Hong Kong, these investors felt they knew their way around China well enough to avoid problems. But instead they landed in the Eighth Circle of Joint-Venture Hell.

It started in 1992, when they entered into a fifty–fifty deal with a company under the local tourism department in Dandong. The local side provided the land and a half-finished shell of a twenty-three-story riverfront building, valued at $4 million. The foreign side matched that amount in cash, which went toward finishing, furnishing, and operating the project.

Business seemed good the first couple of years, but somehow profits were not forthcoming. Accountants were called, and the foreign investors discovered that their partner had falsified company documents to transfer millions of dollars of preexisting debt onto the books of the joint venture.

Lawrence Liu, one of the foreign investors, recounted how creditors they had never heard of came around demanding repayment of loans they never knew about. Eventually, the size of the debts exceeded the registered value of the venture, and the hotel was placed into receivership. The foreign investors, meanwhile, were forcibly ejected from the premises by local police.

They spent years in court, at both the city and provincial level. At every turn, they were convinced that the courts were working hand in glove with their partners. In desperation, they made their way to Beijing seeking intervention from the Ministry of Commerce and other central government departments, but all to no avail. More desperate still, they decided to go public. They told their story to journalists and even mounted public demonstrations, unfurling protest banners on the streets of Beijing.

Finally, in late 2004, they won a ruling that absolved the joint venture of responsibility for the old debts. But far from marking the end of their ordeal, that ruling instead marked the starting point of a new struggle to get it enforced. It took them another year before their stake in the hotel was finally restored, and according to Liu that was possible only because the judge and the interim receivership manager both came under corruption investigations for a range of other scams. But even after regaining access to the hotel, the investors had to struggle with the hostility of the local authorities. In late 2006, Liu accused them of cutting off the hotel's access to hot water and thereby forcing a shutdown.

Dramatic though it is, this tale is hardly unique. Joint ventures large and small have ended up in similar disarray. I have reported on this and other cases myself, and you have no doubt read about still others in the business press. Between all the bad publicity and all the genuine flaws inherent in the format, it is not surprising that joint ventures have become less popular in recent years. In 2000, JVs in their various forms accounted for nearly 52 percent of China's utilized foreign investment. That figure had dropped to 32 percent within four years.

But despite all the risks and all their shortcomings, joint ventures still have their place. In many cases, a well-chosen Chinese partner can deliver benefits that a foreign player would need a lot of time and cash to match. These can range from vital government contacts and support to access to land, distribution channels, qualified workers, sourcing networks, or business licenses in restricted sectors.

Joint Ventures in China

Pitfalls

Unrealistic expectations, poor communication, mismatched goals, misreading the reliability or integrity of a potential partner.

Upside

Can deliver benefits that a foreign player would need a lot of time and cash to match, including government contacts and support as well as access to land, distribution channels, bank credit, qualified workers, or business licenses.

The first step before taking the plunge, then, is to take a clear-eyed look at whether those advantages are worth the potential dilution of control and exposure to the well-known risks.

If the answer is yes, the next step is to exercise maximum caution in the choice of a partner. As the Dandong hotel case shows, misreading the reliability or integrity of a potential partner is all too easy—even for ethnically Chinese investors such as Lawrence Liu and his colleagues, who had the advantage of knowing the language and the culture.

In addition to gauging the baseline integrity of potential partners, you will need to verify their ability to deliver on their end of the deal. If, for example, it is their business license that is the key attraction to your company, you will want to verify that it is valid rather than relying solely on their word. If they are providing hard-to-get land, you will need to ensure that it really is theirs to offer. Even if they are not seeking to scam you outright, they may be overextending themselves.

Chapter 5 provides a lot more detail on how to find this and other kinds of information. Or how to *try* to find it, at least. As you will read in that chapter, complete and reliable information is still hard to come by, despite the vast strides toward openness that China has made in recent years.

The most rigorous attempt at due diligence can still leave you lacking vital information and force you at the end of the day to rely on a gut feeling instead. Even if you've learned to trust your instincts at home, remember that they can easily steer you wrong on unfamiliar terrain.

For yet another cautionary tale, consider what happened to one American investor who, after more than a decade of China experience, led a group that invested $2.5 million into a joint venture to produce trucks in a city in central China.

The group did its homework and felt comfortable with their choice of partner, which was a subsidiary of a leading Chinese automotive firm. This subsidiary was to provide land for the factory as its share of the investment into the venture.

"Prior due diligence? We thought we did it, we had no doubts," the lead investor told me. And after a lavish ceremony marking the establishment of the venture, they had little reason to expect the kind of problems they would soon encounter.

"The opening ceremony was beautiful: They had a banquet and orchestras and lion dancers, and the mayor of the city drove up in a huge black limo. The city government and the partner were all there."

But not long after the banquets and the champagne toasts, the provincial-level government intervened, saying the local partner did not have rights to the land after all. So instead of making trucks and hiring sales people to sell them, the group ended up camping in a hotel for a month and hiring a team of lawyers. Only after a full year of hard haggling did they manage to get their money back.

"It was very frustrating," the lead investor told me. "The timing had been right and the truck business was booming. I expected to spend that time making a success out of this venture, and instead for one whole year I did nothing but fight just to get out of it without losing everything."

Risks like this can be minimized with a cooperative joint venture (CJV) rather than an equity joint venture (EJV). In a CJV, voting rights, staffing decisions, board composition, and other detailed management issues are negotiated up front. Your level of control is thus determined by what you negotiate, and is not tied to any equity ratios.

By contrast, in the typical EJV negotiation partners focus more on the valuation of their capital contributions. Overall, the CJV gives the foreign partner a chance at retaining more control without necessarily injecting huge amounts of capital.

The setup process for a CJV can take longer, but many lawyers will tell you that this is actually an advantage in its own way, since potentially contentious issues are confronted early. By resolving them at this stage, future problems can be averted. Perhaps more importantly, if there are issues that cannot be resolved, it is far better to find that out now.

In addition to reducing the chances of conflict or misunderstanding later, the very process also means that those agreed operational and management details are part of the overall package that goes to government regulators for project approval. So in this situation, investors stand a better chance of finding out ahead of time about problems with partners' ability to deliver what they promise.

Having read this far, you should already know how arbitrary the Chinese system can be, and that these added protections offer no ironclad guarantees. Still, it's that much harder for local partners to wriggle out of obligations if they were built in, documented, and approved from the beginning.

Another big advantage of CJVs is that they offer a way around restrictions against foreign ownership of certain assets. In the mining and energy sectors, for example, foreign entities are generally prohibited from taking direct ownership of Chinese resource assets, even within the confines of an equity joint venture with a local partner. As a Chinese entity, though, the CJV can hold a stake, and the foreign partner can participate through contractual means rather than as an equity shareholder.

Lastly, if things do go bad in a CJV, you will have at least avoided the frustration of having to fight to get your capital back.

Of course, many Chinese enterprises still look to foreign investors for cash first and foremost. But plenty of others are willing to partner on this basis because they know you have other things that they need instead, such as technology, marketing expertise, and management know-how.

GOING IT ALONE

To the great delight of many old-time China hands, it is now possible to bypass entirely the ordeal of finding, vetting, and negotiating with a local partner. The wholly foreign-owned enterprise (WFOE) is far simpler to set up and far easier to control. It was in the early and mid-1990s that this structure became available. But it really began to take off after 2001, when China's WTO accession compelled it to do away with more restrictions on the activities of foreign business.

Commonly referred to as a "Wofie" (pronounced *woe fee*), the WFOE format was mainly introduced to facilitate foreign investment in manufacturing and processing ventures aimed at the export market. Vestiges of that policy choice remain today in the generous tax breaks given to WFOEs that produce entirely for export.

A WFOE is technically a limited liability company that is entirely owned by one or more foreign entities. While it is possible for foreign firms to partner with each other to create a jointly owned WFOE, this isn't commonly done. Instead, most WFOEs are owned by a single foreign firm.

Since 2003, the rules have loosened considerably in terms of what WFOEs may produce for local consumption, but in general those that do sell domestically continue to face higher tax burdens. For example, their imported components are not eligible for the duty refunds that exporting WFOEs can usually obtain.

While your 100 percent ownership of a WFOE can free you from the hassles of a local partner, it can also deprive you of some of the benefits, most significantly a local presence with good connections and a solid understanding of the local environment. That can make a WFOE a poor choice for anyone very new to China.

Even for investors who are relatively familiar with the country, and who have taken care to hire suitably well-positioned local managers, a WFOE will not likely be able to match the institutional clout that a local JV partner can usually provide. You will instead be seen as the all-foreign entity that you are, and—notwithstanding all the WTO-mandated requirements of equal national treatment that China has agreed to—that can put you at a distinct disadvantage when it comes to competing with domestic players.

More recently, China has allowed another type of WFOE structure that allows foreigners to conduct trading or selling activities rather than assembly or manufacture. Called FICEs (foreign invested commercial enterprises), these are seeing more approvals all the time. As a form of a WFOE, a FICE can allow you to enter into retailing, wholesaling, or even franchising operations without a local partner. In many cases, FICEs can be approved solely at the local level without any involvement from central government officials at the Ministry of Commerce. In some cases, though, such as a proposed FICE dealing with the distribution of strategic raw materials or one operating in a restricted industry, ministry approval from Beijing is still required.

MAXIMUM SIMPLICITY, MINIMUM OUTLAY

As the simplest option of all, you might consider opening a representative office in China. Among its chief limitations, a representative office cannot invoice within China for goods or services. It is also somewhat restricted in terms of how staff are hired and where its premises need to be located. But for a wide range of purposes, it can be surprisingly flexible. Indeed, in the early stages especially, it could be all you need.

For a lot of companies, a small rep office is the preferred way to quickly and easily establish an initial presence in China.

If, for example, you want to conduct preliminary market research, a rep office can give you a way to rent office space, hire staff, and obtain residence permits for yourself or other foreign employees. Setup can usually be accomplished within a couple of months, but bear in mind that for all its simplicity, the rep office structure does generate tax liabilities.

Despite the prohibition on invoicing, the rep office can also be scaled up to a very substantial level. If, for example, you are selling imported commodities or capital equipment manufactured in the United States, your sales contracts can be conducted between the end user and your parent company. But your marketing, sales, and service staffs can all be based out of your rep office.

A rep office can also be a way to base your quality control operations and purchasing staff if you are sourcing products in China.

COPYRIGHTS AND COPY WRONGS

Apart from the issues related to structuring a China project, the single greatest legal concern is probably the country's poor state of intellectual property rights (IPR) enforcement and protection. It is a massive, and seemingly intractable, problem, and it's hard to name a sector that does not feel the impact. Some of the most conspicuous violators are the pirates selling Hollywood movies and the latest pop music throughout China for $1 or less per CD or DVD. I need only walk a hundred yards from my office to find a wide selection of recent releases, and if I walk just a little farther, I can also shop for illegal knockoff versions of Armani shirts for $5 each, Nike shoes for $10 a pair, and Louis Vuitton purses, Samsonite suitcases, or Burberry coats for $20 apiece. Indeed, it is hard to say which is more mind-boggling: the variety of fake products on offer, or the brazenness of the producers and vendors who sell them.

According to US officials, an estimated 90 percent of all DVDs and software in the China market are illegal. China, as they point out, is the world's second largest market for personal computers, but only the twenty-fifth largest for the basic software that they use.

But the problem runs at a far deeper level than the software or the luxury-brand ripoffs you can find as you stroll down any Beijing street. Food products, medicines, and car parts are just a few of the thousands of other products that are counterfeited in China, and in addition to the economic costs, fakes like these pose real health and safety risks to consumers.

Another disturbing aspect of the IPR issue is that vast quantities of counterfeit goods are now making their way into the export stream. The US Commerce Department estimates that two-thirds of the fake goods seized by US Customs authorities originate in China. The European Union and Japan report similar ratios. Companies are therefore dealing with more than a threat to their share of the China market. They now face damage to their reputation in markets around the world, and must even worry about liability exposure because of substandard products that are now circulating under their name. Overall, according to commerce officials, counterfeiting and piracy cost American business upward of $200 billion each year.

Western governments, including that of the United States, have for years been pressing China to improve its laws and enforcement in the IPR realm. The pressure is rising from within now, too, because more and more Chinese businesses have IPR interests of their own to defend. Some of the most extreme measures have been taken by China's most famous film directors, like Zhang Yimou and Chen Kaige. In an effort to protect their recent films, these directors have gone to such lengths as sleeping with their master reels by their pillow or hiring armed guards. Opening-night audiences have been checked with metal detectors and monitored with night-vision gear as they watched. Even with all this, Chen, Zhang and other artists know they can at best only delay illicit copying for a short initial interval.

China shows signs of taking the issue seriously. As it often does with other big legal problems, the government has launched periodic crackdowns, with highly publicized raids on markets and factories. Chinese newscasts seem never to tire of showing footage of police bulldozers crushing thousands of seized CDs and DVDs. But for pirates, the occasional raid, fine, or loss of inventory is merely a cost of business, and they quickly find their way back into operation.

Experts say progress is coming, but warn that it will be slow. For Chinese government officials, especially at the local level, IPR protection stands little chance of making it to the top of anyone's list of priorities. Pirates may be breaking the law and harming the interests of legitimate businesses as well as China's reputation. But they are also providing jobs, and probably even paying some tax. Compared with the pressing array of other problems that a typical Chinese official has to deal with, this one is not likely to scream out for attention.

But for a foreign company that falls victim to Chinese product counterfeiting, the issue can become a dismaying and resource-draining priority. One such firm is the Will-Burt Company. Based in Orrville, Ohio, Will-Burt manufactures a variety of products, including a telescoping light mast specially designed for police and other emergency vehicles. The company contracted with a Chinese partner in Guangdong Province to distribute the lighting systems in China. Sales rose steadily at first to more than $1 million a year, but then suddenly began a decline, halving year by year and eventually dwindling down to almost nothing, according to Will-Burt CEO Jeffrey Evans.

The company quickly discovered that its partner had blatantly copied the product design—together with logos and technical manuals, without even bothering to remove the Will-Burt Web address—and started manufacturing and selling it in China at cut-rate prices. In testimony before Congress, Evans said it was particularly ironic that Will-Burt's end customer, the Chinese national police agency, had been purchasing illegal counterfeit products from Chinese companies that were directly violating laws that they should have been enforcing.

Even more alarming, though, may be the fact that Will-Burt was aware of the danger and took precautions, doing everything it thought it could from the start. "I don't know what else we could have done," Evans told me. "We had patents, trademarks, confidentiality agreements, noncompete clauses. If you can't avoid an illegal sale with those precautions in place, I'm not sure where you can go next."

AN UPHILL STRUGGLE FIT FOR SISYPHUS

There may be no Westerner who knows more about China's IPR problems than Mark Cohen. An experienced China hand and longtime IPR attorney, Cohen joined the US Patent and Trademark Office and was in 2004 seconded to the US embassy in Beijing as the first American patent official ever posted overseas. His assignment—monitoring China's IPR environment, prodding the Chinese government toward better standards and enforcement, and advising US firms on how to protect their interests—is not for the faint of heart. Quite appropriately, the *Wall Street Journal* once called it "a job fit for Sisyphus."

But for all the discouragement he faces, Cohen insists that American companies *can* take steps to minimize their exposure and increase their chances in China's IPR jungle. One key, he told me, is avoiding the biggest mistake that many companies make, which is to assume that the system in China works like it does in the United States. "If you come in here assuming that intellectual property rights are defined the same way or enforced the same ways, you are wrong on both counts," he said.

He urges US companies to take advantage of what the Chinese system does offer. For example, design patents and Chinese-language trademarks can be registered in China at only a modest cost. Doing so provides no guarantee of protection, as the Will-Burt case amply illustrates. But it will provide a better basis for legal or administrative action down the road, especially as the Chinese government's slow-moving efforts proceed.

Cohen also warns that legal responses have to be chosen carefully and focused in localities where they might make a difference, typically in China's larger cities. He urges companies to team up within industries to coordinate and maximize the pressure they bring to bear on legal and administrative systems.

Some IPR experts propose widening the attack to take on other actors in the pirating and fake-products industry. Having grown tired of going after producers and vendors with little to show for their efforts, some foreign companies have instead begun to pursue the landlords who allow their rented market space to be used for the sale of illegal products. At the end of 2005, for example, a group of companies including Chanel, Gucci, and Prada won a Beijing court ruling that penalized the owners at one of Beijing's most prominent market stalls. Even though the amount of the settlement was more a token than a deterrent, and even though pirated goods promptly made their way back to the same market stalls, this does represent a new and promising angle of attack.

The US embassy in Beijing maintains an online "IPR Toolkit" on its Web site (http://beijing.usembassy-china.org.cn/protecting_ipr.html) that contains more current and detailed information on what companies can do to protect themselves. Another useful resource is the Quality Brands Protection Committee, a multi-industry business association with more than 140 multinational members representing an estimated $50 billion worth of foreign investment into China (www .qbpc.org.cn).

KEY POINTS TO REMEMBER
FROM CHAPTER 2

1. For a country with a well-earned reputation as a harsh police state, China is often surprisingly—and distressingly—lawless. This paradox presents a potential minefield for foreign business people. Furthermore, laws change at an astonishing rate. So regardless of how much you already know about China, you will need professional legal help on an ongoing basis.

2. China's legal system is becoming increasingly accessible at all levels. From the legislature to the courts, ordinary citizens and foreign business people alike can find ways to offer input into the lawmaking process and seek redress for problems. The system's performance remains spotty, but you should not discount the possibility that you can make it work for you.

3. Enforcement of existing laws is often lax in China, but you cannot assume you will get away with anything.

Foreigners are often treated more leniently than locals, but not always.

4. The choice of how to structure your venture is crucial. There are now more choices than ever before, and many foreign investors are delighted at not having to go the joint-venture route. It is now easy to establish wholly foreign-owned enterprises in China. But for some businesses the simplest option, a representative office, may suffice.

5. The joint-venture structure carries huge risk and usually guarantees a fair amount of frustration with the behavior of the local partner. But in many cases, a carefully selected partner can deliver benefits that the foreign partner could only match with a lot of effort and a lot of cash, if at all. The potential access to land, distribution channels, business licenses, qualified workers, sourcing networks, and government support may well be worth the risk.

6. China's IPR regime is an absolute jungle, and while there are steps that companies can take to try to protect themselves, there is no guarantee they will be effective. Any product, from software to shoes to machinery, can and likely will be knocked off in China, and many companies quickly find themselves competing with cut-rate versions of their own products. Experts expect to see progress, especially as more and more Chinese stakeholders get hurt by piracy but they warn that it will take time.

3

Cultural Differences and Etiquette

Economists and politicians can argue endlessly about whether China is "different" or "unique." Some maintain that with its vast population and landmass, its jackrabbit pace of development, its grandiose imperial heritage, and its growing modern-day clout, China is simply in a class of its own. The natural follow-up to that view is that the outside world must fashion new and uniquely tailored modes of dealing with the unprecedented rise of such a player onto the world stage.

Others look at China and insist there is nothing entirely unique about it. India is booming, too, after all, and it is nearly as large. In fact, the United Nations projects that India's population will surpass China's by midcentury. Other economies, in East Asia and elsewhere, have grown as fast as China's.

And history tells of many big powers that elbowed their way to the center of the international order as soon as their wealth, political influence, and military might allowed them to do so.

In this view, China today can be compared to Japan, the United States, or Germany, among others. Each of those, for better or worse, made waves in the world order as it rose to big-power status. So while dealing with a rising China will require careful and strategic thinking, there is nothing here that the world has not seen before, and there is no need to treat it as a special case.

The debate is bound to continue long into the future. But there can be no debating this: When it comes to culture, norms of etiquette, social behavior, and political sensitivities, China is unique. At the same time, it is changing fast, so even for Chinese people who have been away for a while, keeping up is hard. Nevertheless, the more you know about its intricate and elaborate norms, the easier it will be to get by in China, and to get things done.

A good grounding in the basics of Chinese etiquette can not only win you some minor points as a charmer, but more importantly provide you valuable insights into the methods, motives, and meanings of the Chinese people you deal with. And while minor lapses of etiquette can usually pass without consequence, a major failure to appreciate common norms and expectations can sour key relationships and add unnecessary friction to your dealings.

Of course, to truly get a feel for these things, there is no substitute for time spent on the ground paying close attention and soaking it all up yourself. But what this chapter can do is help get you started in understanding what you need to know.

IS CHIVALRY DEAD?

At a certain level, etiquette is actually becoming somewhat less important in China than it used to be. Part of the change is generational. Among older people, you will find traditional attitudes very much in place, and when dealing with them matters of etiquette remain important. This applies especially to people who continue to work in old-line state-owned enterprises or some of the more hidebound government ministries.

But just as in other societies, China's younger people tend to be considerably less formal than their elders, more open to outside influences, and in general more easygoing. As a foreigner, you will find interaction with these people to be far less stilted.

One reason is simply a lot more exposure to the outside world than any previous generation. China's urban youth are avid consumers of Western popular culture. Although they don't often pay for legal genuine versions of it, they do widely enjoy Western pop music, American TV shows, and Hollywood movies. Regardless of whether these media offerings transmit an accurate picture of Western life, the exposure to them has undoubtedly provided a view of alternative cultures, as well as the understanding that Western social norms differ from China's.

More substantially, a lot of the people you deal with are themselves likely to have traveled abroad—sometimes extensively. Many, in fact, will have spent years studying in the United States, Australia, or Europe. In the tech industries, you will find that many have even worked abroad for Western companies, ranging from top-tier multinationals to tiny Silicon Valley start-ups. With all this experience under their belts, they are plenty accustomed to dealing with foreigners, and adjusting to foreign corporate cultures, too. They are hardly likely to be put off by any failure of yours to properly execute Chinese manners.

"Things have changed," Andy Rothman, a Shanghai-based China strategist with brokerage house CLSA Asia-Pacific, told me. "It used to be that business in China was done with high officials only. But now, 70 percent of China's economy and 80 percent of its enterprises are small and medium enterprises. Things are often done enterprise-to-enterprise, and these are entrepreneurs very much like the people you're used to dealing with elsewhere."

On several levels, the vastly broader outlook of people like this is a good leading indicator of just how much contemporary China has evolved. From my point of view, it calls to mind some of my own clumsy social moments in my early days in China going back to 1989. In an innocent attempt to chat about something I could handle with my still-middling Chinese skills, I would often ask people whether they had ever been to the United States.

The answer was just about always no, and it took me longer than it probably should have to realize why that was—and more importantly, why the responses always seemed so awkward.

Some senior-level officials back then would have had the chance to go abroad at some point in their career, often to someplace in the Soviet bloc, but possibly to the United States as well. A lot of doctors and scientists had by that time also had opportunities to study in the West.

But for just about anyone else, the odds were pretty slim, so much so that they would consider the very question ridiculous. (In a similar vein, I also learned early on to stop asking people how many kids they had. To people bristling under a strict one-child population control policy, my friendly question actually came off sounding more like some kind of cruel joke.)

Another indicator of the changes taking place in China is the common reaction of Chinese people who do spend time abroad and then come back. Many of them say they feel like strangers in their own hometowns. Part of it is simply the pace of new construction. Returnees can hardly find their way around on all the new roads, and can hardly recognize the once familiar neighborhoods that have been utterly transformed.

But more than that, they feel left behind by the way the culture is changing. From the political scene to the latest trends and fads, and even new vocabulary, they find much in their own country that is unfamiliar.

HEY, LOOK! A FOREIGNER!

Whatever difficulties these returnees may have in readjusting, however, cannot compare to the situation you will face when you spend any amount of time in China.

Foreigners, no matter how good their Chinese-language abilities, no matter how long they've lived in the country, and no matter how thoroughly they've mastered the subtleties of Chinese etiquette, will always be viewed as outsiders and categorized accordingly.

Among the first words of Chinese you are likely to learn will be the phrase *lao wai*. It is literally translated as "old foreigner," but in fact it has nothing to do with age. It is simply the common vernacular term used to refer to a foreigner. Not exactly derogatory, it's not quite affectionate, either. It is more like an unabashed statement of the obvious, and if you pay attention, you will hear it muttered in your presence all the time.

Little children will point their fingers and yell it out as you pass by. Grown men may be less likely to point and yell, but they will often say it all the same upon seeing you, as if reflexively. It is simply a measure of how your foreignness stands out as your dominant trait.

As an extreme example, consider a remarkable gentleman named Sidney Shapiro. A Brooklyn-born lawyer, he moved to China in the 1940s, married a local woman, started a family, and in the 1960s became a Chinese citizen. With his virtually native-level Chinese, he has made a career for himself as an author and literary translator, and he even holds a prestigious position in the Chinese government's top advisory body, the Chinese People's Political Consultative Conference. He has lived for decades in the same traditional courtyard home in the alleyways of central Beijing.

All this notwithstanding, when I was trying to find his home some years ago, his friendly and helpful neighbors were quick to ask whether I was looking for "that foreigner's house" and then point me in the right direction.

My own family is another good case in point. My wife, who is American, has lived in Beijing since 1979. I arrived in 1989, our three children have lived their entire lives here, and any of us can get a fair way into a telephone conversation in Chinese before we give ourselves away as foreigners. But upon meeting local people in person, we are immediately and irretrievably pegged as foreigners. And everything about us is then seen through that prism.

After spending any length of time in China, you will quickly come to feel that your foreignness is taken as your sole defining trait, and as wearing as that can sometimes be, it also has its advantages. Many foreign women in business, for example, feel that their gender is less of an issue in China than it is at home, simply because the fact that they are foreign tends to blot out everything else.

Another advantage is that, as a foreigner, you are not necessarily expected to understand the intricacies of Chinese etiquette, and so you will be granted considerable leeway for any lapses. Against these lowered expectations, you can easily score valuable points when you get things right.

BIG STUFF AND SMALL STUFF

When it comes to etiquette in China, there is a vital distinction to be made between the grand and the petty, or what I call the Big Stuff and the Small Stuff.

With the Big Stuff, you can make damaging mistakes if you inadvertently slight the wrong person, violate protocol, embarrass an important counterpart, or put people on the spot when it comes to politics.

On the Small Stuff side of the ledger, there are certain niceties that are worth knowing about and practicing, but in the end they are just what that term implies: nice, and little more. It's very unlikely that your handling of a minor point of etiquette will ever make or break a deal.

In fact, I have a minor confession to make at this point. I am constantly bemused at the sight of Western business people who come to China thinking that so long as they know to exchange name cards with two hands, everything is under control.

If you have done any reading at all about business in China, you have probably seen this gem revealed as if it is some kind of ancient Chinese secret. You might well hear it from the person sitting next to you on the flight over. A typical example of this oracular revelation appeared in 2005, in the British newspaper the *Guardian:* "In China, accept business cards with two hands, like they're the most precious thing you've ever been given, a wise friend told me."

Well, dear grasshopper, that is not exactly *bad* advice. But it may be the single most overrated and overexposed piece of China wisdom out there. Yes, it is true that taking or giving a card with two hands is considered a formal and polite gesture. Many Chinese people will take the trouble to do it, and if you are meeting very high-ranking people it is especially appropriate for you to do it, too.

In fact, you can go ahead and make it your practice to use the two-hand rule all the time. While you are at it, you may as well follow it up with the corollary: Upon receiving someone's card, you should not casually slip it into your pocket without a glance. Instead, you should spend a moment looking it over, and perhaps even show your interest by making a comment about some detail, such as the building or the neighborhood shown in the address.

It will also be worth your while to take some care in choosing the Chinese version of your name. Many Westerners simply end up with a name that uses Chinese syllables to make a rough approximation of the sound. But these often strike Chinese people as nonsensical and difficult to remember. You can make a better impression by choosing characters that bear some relationship to the sound of your name but also work well in Chinese terms. Most Chinese names consist of three characters, with the first one denoting the family name and the second two denoting the given name. A good start would be to choose a standard Chinese surname in which the first letter matches that of your own. With the next two characters, you can also aim to include some of the sounds of your own given name, but make sure their meaning is pleasing. The selection of a good Chinese name is far more an art than a science, and it will pay to solicit advice from any literary-minded Chinese acquaintances. Take some time to select a name you like, and then pay attention to the reaction it garners. Once you do settle on a name, it is a good idea to stick with it, as it will be a key part of your identity in the minds of the Chinese people you deal with.

What you must remember, though, is that none of this is any kind of magic key to success. If your business is fundamentally sound, your violation of name card etiquette is not going to sink you. And if it's not, your mastery of that etiquette won't save you, either.

The Big Stuff, the Small Stuff, and the Little Things

In matters of Chinese etiquette, watch out for the Big Stuff—issues and missteps that can really cost you. These include slighting a senior official, ignoring considerations of face, embarrassing a counterpart, losing your temper, and raising delicate political topics at the wrong time or place. Mistakes like these can cause you lasting harm.

Be aware of the Small Stuff—but don't worry too much about it. You can score some valuable points by mastering certain forms of etiquette in banquet situations, gift giving, and the handling of name cards. But a clumsy performance is not likely to cause you much grief.

And don't ignore the Little Things! These are issues that may seem trivial to you but can be very important to your Chinese counterparts. Be on time for meetings, don't ask people to skip meals, and be aware of holidays on the Chinese calendar.

Banquet etiquette falls into a similar category. There are plenty of ready tidbits that will serve you well if you observe them. For example, you should not begin eating until your host has formally started the meal, usually with a simple toast. You should avoid putting your chopsticks all over the common food. If you are the host, put some food on your guest's plate before serving yourself. And if you want to get really fancy, you can even flip your chopsticks around when you do it, so you are not using the end that has been in your mouth.

The list goes on and on. Some of it is perfectly intuitive for a Westerner. If you are pouring tea or wine, fill the cups of others before you fill your own. It is not polite to take the last piece of food from a common plate.

Other things are less intuitive. If using a toothpick, for example, the common practice in China is to wield the tooth-pick with one hand while cupping your other hand over your face to keep your teeth and open mouth out of view. Oddly enough, though, many Chinese people have no qualms about picking their noses in public—consider the contrast a testa-ment to the arbitrary nature of manners everywhere.

Similarly, many Chinese have no compunction at all about loudly hawking up copious amounts of phlegm and then spit-ting it on the ground, wherever they happen to be. It is some-times even done indoors, although this is thankfully becoming less common. A lot of Westerners find this very disconcerting. But cringe though they might at the sight and sound of it, they should also be aware that Chinese find it equally off-putting to see Westerners blowing their noses into hankies that they put back into their pockets.

In gift giving, it is the common Chinese custom for the recipient to politely refuse an offering as many as three times. So you should be careful not to back off and withdraw the gift after the first refusal, because you will create an awkward situation by short-circuiting the ritual. Once the recipient has accepted a gift, do not be surprised (or offended) if he or she takes it without opening it in front of you. It is simply the Chinese convention to do it this way. That said, there is nothing wrong with inviting the recipient to open it on the spot.

There are also standard rituals involving apologies and compliments. At meals, Chinese hosts will frequently berate their own offerings and apologize for the paucity of it all. In fact, this is a common form of false modesty, and your host will be mildly offended if you accept the apology at face value. The appropriate response is to instead bat down the apology and offer lavish praise on how impressive and abundant the spread really is.

Yet another Chinese ritual comes into play at the end of a visit. Whether it's a visit to a home or an office, most Chinese will not simply pack you off at the door. Instead, they will often accompany you to the street or the main gate of the building or compound, then wait until you get into your car, waving good-bye nonstop until you have driven out of sight.

Depending on the formality of the situation, this gesture is sometimes diluted in practice, and you might just be accompanied to the elevator. Even in this case, though, your host will stay with you until the elevator comes, and keep waving good-bye right until those doors slide shut. As with all these practices, you will not go wrong if you give your guests the same treatment. You will, of course, have to disregard them when they repeatedly insist there is no need to send them off.

It is also a Chinese custom for the recipient of applause to applaud back at the crowd. It doesn't matter whether it's a performer onstage in a large venue, a speaker taking the podium, or a prominent person entering a room. If you find yourself in a situation where people are clapping for you, ignore how strange it feels and just clap right back.

For a lot of these minor matters of etiquette, your best bet is pay close attention, watch what people do, and take your cues from them. You won't go far wrong this way. And even if you do, remember: *This is the Small Stuff.* You may leave people quietly thinking how strange it is that foreigners lack basic manners, but they are not likely to be surprised—or to hold it against you.

THE BIG STUFF

What you should really be paying attention to is the Big Stuff. This is where you can either help yourself or hurt yourself in truly significant ways. It includes such issues as managing your relationships with local people, understanding the unique Chinese conventions of communication, and Chinese negotiating styles. It also concerns the Chinese style of exchanging favors and the special sensitivities of discussing politics.

Relationships: Who's Who?

Managing relationships will be one of your key challenges, and one size definitely does not fit all. You will need to adjust your comportment when dealing with staff, negotiating counterparts, and bureaucrats. The first step is understanding who is who—and especially who is the boss.

For the uninitiated, it can be hard to remember Chinese names and faces. Every meeting will leave you with a stack of name cards, and for a lot of non-Chinese-speakers, it can be hard to make sense of all the *Z*'s and *Q*'s and *X*'s in the names. It doesn't help that a handful of Chinese surnames are incredibly common. Believe it or not, there are more than a hundred million people in China surnamed *Li*. The surnames *Chen, Zhang, Liu,* and *Wang* are almost as common.

To add to the potential confusion, many Chinese given names are also made up of a relatively small set of characters and similar-sounding syllables. You should also remember that Chinese surnames come first, and, with only a few rare exceptions, they are only one syllable. Given names come second, and can be made up of either one or two syllables. So in the case of Chinese President Hu Jintao, the surname is *Hu* and the given name is *Jintao*. Should you ever have the chance to meet him then, the appropriate form of address would be "President Hu," *not* "President Jintao." (And in the highly unlikely event he were to offer you his name card, it would be an excellent idea to receive it with two hands!)

As you'll read in chapter 7, learning Chinese is actually a lot easier than you probably think. But even if you cannot manage to learn any of the language, you should at least achieve enough basic familiarity with the sounds and the transliteration conventions to allow you to remember and pronounce the names of people and places.

It is at least as important to learn how to differentiate titles. Anyone who gives you a name card is putting this vital information directly in your hand, almost always with an English translation on one side of the card. There is really no excuse for not grasping it. But there can be consequences.

A failure to understand the hierarchy of Chinese groups you meet with can be disastrous, especially if it results in a failure to give proper recognition to the senior figure on the opposite side of the table. I have noticed over the years that Russians who came of age in the Soviet era are among the foreigners with the best intuitive knack for understanding who is who in formal Chinese settings, thanks to the similarities between the Chinese and Soviet party-led bureaucracies. Even though you lack that advantage, you nevertheless need to make sure you know who the boss is.

Within the government bureaucracy, the ministry (called *bu* in Chinese) is the highest-level agency, followed by the bureau (*ju*) and the department (*si*). In Chinese, the head official in any of these, whether a man or a woman, is designated by the suffix *zhang*, which means "head" or "chief." So a minister is a *buzhang*, a bureau director is a *juzhang*, and a department head is called a *sizhang*. Coming after the words for province, city, district or county, the *zhang* suffix denotes a governor, mayor, district chief, or county boss, respectively.

Most of these agencies will also have several deputy heads, and these are denoted by the prefix *fu*, meaning "vice" or "secondary." By way of flattery, people in China will commonly engage in some subtle rank inflation by omitting that prefix when addressing a deputy-level official. So if you are meeting with Vice Mayor Wang, you will hear everyone call him "Mayor Wang." He would no doubt be pleased to hear you refer to him the same way.

When they get down to brass tacks, though, and really need to know who is who, the Chinese are very clear about rankings. They dispense with the generous flattery of rank inflation and are instead very careful to distinguish between, say, a mayor and a vice mayor. When preparing to receive a group from another organization, whether Chinese or foreign, they will ask for a lot of advance information.

In providing this kind of information themselves, Chinese organizations carefully list all members in order of rank. (They also commonly assume that any such list you give to them is ordered on the same basis, so you will create a lot of confusion if you submit a list in alphabetical order!)

Another important thing to remember is that every Chinese organization has a parallel hierarchy of Communist party officials. In some cases, one big boss will head both the administrative and party structures. But when that is not the case, you must remember that it is almost always the party boss who trumps the administrative leader. At the very top of the Chinese government, for example, that means that Hu Jintao, as general secretary of the party, is the real top dog. The head of the government, Prime Minister Wen Jiabao, actually ranks third in the party leadership. And it is the party ranking that really counts.

Another very common mistake that Westerners make in China is to gravitate toward the best English speaker in any group. It is a perfectly natural tendency, since this may be the only person you can relate to and communicate with on any substantial level. But it can also end up distorting your priorities.

Although English ability may make someone stand out in your mind, that is not necessarily the person you should be focusing your attention on. This is especially true since many good English speakers tend to be younger, while your real target is likely to be a more senior person. The people who by rank are actually your parallel counterparts may very well feel slighted at the sight of excessive chumminess between you and one of their far younger underlings.

Relationships: What's What?

Once you have figured out who is who, what is it that you need to know to keep things smooth, friendly, and productive? In any relationship, at any level, two very important concepts are always in play. As is the case with name card etiquette, they are both widely talked about by Westerners, and you have perhaps already been advised as to their importance. The difference, though, is that unlike name cards, these really do matter in a big way.

One is "face," usually called *mianzi* in Chinese. The other is *guanxi*, broadly (but incompletely) translatable as "connections." And both are very highly valued commodities in China.

Face: The Facts

The Chinese concept of face is a profoundly rich and nuanced subject, but if you want to boil it down to its simplest terms you can think of it as the sum total of what is publicly visible about a person. In short, it is his or her reputation.

With that in mind, it is not so hard to understand the ways that face can be given, lost, or saved. Anything you do to make people look good or enhance their standing is to give them face. And anything you do to make people look bad causes them to lose face.

It should not be an entirely alien concept for Westerners. After all, isn't it just basic human nature to want to look good, and have others think well of you? What is different about it in China is the way the notion of face has been codified into an elaborate and explicit social construct, and the extent to which it is emphasized. For most Westerners, the sense of face may be present as a steady background concern, but it is not usually front and center in their thinking. For most Chinese, by contrast, it tends to be a primary concern, consciously weighed and carefully measured all the time.

In fact, there are gradations of face. The most common everyday form is *mianzi*. But for more grave matters, the terminology changes—what is lost is not *mianzi*, but *lian*. If, for example, your spouse is seen bickering with you in public, it is thought to reflect badly on you and results in a loss of *mianzi*. But if your spouse is known to have taken a lover, then things are much worse, and you have lost *lian*.

In the context of business, most negotiations eventually turn into questions of face. As a simple illustration, imagine you are out in one of Beijing's many clothing markets, talking to a stall keeper about a cashmere sweater that has caught your eye. In the early stages, the negotiating hinges on the value of the thing itself. The vendor tells you that his high asking price is justified by the exquisite quality of the material and the excellent workmanship.

Soon other people start paying attention to the negotiation, and gradually your offer rises while his asking price drops. By now, the difference is down to a trivial amount. You give your final offer, he refuses it, and you start to walk away. Then the vendor calls you back and asks that you add just a small amount more to your final offer, in order to "give him a little face."

And with that, the final decision is up to you. Because with a crowd looking on, the vendor would probably prefer to lose the sale than be seen to lose the showdown by agreeing to your final offer instead of getting you to move off it.

This psychological gamesmanship occurs all the way up and down the line, from the largest and most complex of deals to the simplest of interpersonal behavior, and at times you may find yourself wondering whether *face* is just a glorified Chinese term for a form of stubborn, childish pride.

But whatever you choose to call it, and whatever you may think of it, you will have to deal with it. And no matter what you are negotiating for, you should plan to leave a little extra room in your "final offer" for that endgame face offering.

Face isn't only a factor in dollars-and-cents negotiations, however. It will be a factor in just about any interaction you have with local people.

Getting Connected: *Guanxi*

Even more than *face,* the full meaning of *guanxi* defies translation into any single English word. The direct translation is simple enough: It means "relationship" or "connection," and the word is often used in that narrow sense. When talking about relations between two countries, for example, *guanxi* is the appropriate word. It is also used in the logical or causal sense to refer, say, to a direct connection between cause X and effect Y.

But when used in terms of doing business and dealing with the bureaucracy, *guanxi* has a far broader meaning, taking in everything from "connections" to "networking" to "pull."

Again, it is not a totally alien concept. In American terms, it can be compared to the idea that success in business depends on "who you know, not what you know." There is no doubt that access to good contacts can be a huge advantage in American business. Whether you are looking to land a job or to close a deal, knowing the right people can help you get a foot in the door or help you make your way up the ladder.

As the countless bribery and influence-peddling scandals in Washington, DC, show all too well, access to government decision makers is a highly prized commodity in America, too. Even so, it is fair to say there are certain limits on how far anyone can ride connections before hitting the wall.

As you saw in chapter 2, though, the restraining walls in China can be pretty flimsy. With such weak laws and institutions, and with so much arbitrary power in the hands of officials, the importance of "who you know" can run far deeper.

Those same conditions are what facilitate the rampant levels of corruption in China that you will read about in chapter 8. Though closely related, *guanxi* and corruption are actually quite different. You can think of *guanxi* as corruption but without material bribery. The favors bestowed may be similar, but the motivation is entirely different.

Plenty of corruption and bribery go on in China, but when *guanxi* is at work, it is a different story. Powerful people are not bending the rules for cash. They are doing it because of the inherent obligations they perceive in their relationships with the recipients of their favors.

The importance of these relationships is ranked hierarchically. At the top are family connections—even distant ones—followed by friendships. People who come from the same town or village will feel a kinship and an obligation to one another. The relationship between school classmates is also surprisingly important; even people who were not especially close during their school days will hold their classmate relationship in very high regard.

You must remember that whenever you make a transaction at the Chinese favor bank, whether as grantor or recipient, the accounting is strict. And unlike small matters of etiquette, Chinese people will generally expect that you understand and play by the rules. This can cut both ways. People coming to you asking for a favor—say, a personal loan, help with a visa, or help in getting a job—fully understand that they are incurring a debt in the form of a reciprocal favor of similar magnitude. And they fully expect you to call it in, even if it is years later. For your part, you must be mindful of the debts you incur when you ask someone to do a favor for you.

For a succinct illustration of how *guanxi* and the favor bank, together with China's capricious legal environment, can determine outcomes, consider a simple business dispute that befell my wife's company some years ago.

The company sold imported lab equipment to an institute in Beijing's university district. The parties had a straightforward sales contract, but long after the equipment was delivered, the purchaser refused to pay the agreed price, around $20,000. The case went to court, where it was handled as a fairly cut-and-dried matter. Having clearly determined that the purchaser had signed a contract and accepted delivery of the equipment, the court ordered it to pay up.

In line with standard Chinese legal procedure, the ruling was then passed along to the district enforcement department. In theory, these departments are responsible for implementing court decisions, and they are empowered to take compulsory measures such as freezing bank accounts, garnishing wages, or ordering the confiscation and sale of property.

But in this case, the enforcement officials declined to move against the purchaser. It was very awkward, they said, because the institute was based in their own district and they were acquainted with the people there. Of course, the very reason the case came to these officials to begin with was that the transaction took place there. It was their jurisdiction! Nevertheless, they said, compelling the institute to pay the judgment "would ruin their relationship," and they simply preferred not to do that. Next case.

Outlandish as that scenario sounds, it is actually quite common in China, in cases involving local as well as foreign litigants. It is estimated that nationwide, no more than 60 percent of monetary judgments are ever enforced. In some of the more backward parts of the country, that figure can be as low as 10 percent, according to one Chinese legal journal.

But luckily for my wife's company, the matter did not quite end there. Neither did the role of *guanxi*. It turned out that the senior partner of her company's law firm was a former classmate of a senior official in the enforcement department. Calls were made, meals were shared, and the judgment was finally enforced. And of course, the lawyer now owed the official a favor. This episode is hardly a ringing endorsement for the effectiveness of the Chinese legal system. But it sure does say a lot about how *guanxi* really works.

Communication: Subtle Signals

One key to navigating successfully through the cloudy realms of face, *guanxi,* and Chinese etiquette is understanding that even the most basic norms of communication in China are very different from what you are used to.

For one thing, people are very reluctant to say no, even if that is what they really mean. It can take a lot of getting used to, and it can take a lot of effort to avoid the feeling that people are being duplicitous or deceptive. But in many cases, this behavior comes from the impulse to avoid an uncomfortable situation and save you the loss of face that—in the Chinese view—would come with asking for something and not getting it. The typical response to a request that cannot be met is a promise to "consider" or "study" it, or to check with superiors. The danger of pushing for a firmer answer is that you can readily force a yes that is in fact noncommittal, and ultimately worthless.

Another unique thing about Chinese modes of communication is a tendency toward literal-mindedness. This means irony and sarcasm are not much practiced, and not well understood. It also means that a specific question will usually get a very specific answer, with no effort to anticipate what other relevant information you might want to know.

Years ago, for example, while I was shopping in a Beijing department store for a coffeepot, the salesclerk displayed her impressive knowledge of the wares, answering every single question I had about all the dozen or so display models. But when I made my choice, she told me they were out of stock. When I chose another, she told me that was out of stock, too. It turned out I had only a couple of choices, and I found it odd that she didn't tell me up front which ones were in stock. But in fact her response was very standard for China. I had asked about features, and she told me about features. I have since learned that the first thing to do in these situations is ask, "Which ones do you have in stock?" and take it from there.

The more general lesson is that Chinese people will not likely volunteer any information you didn't ask for, so if you ever think, *They would have told me if that was the case!*— you are almost certainly wrong.

Complicated? You Bet!

One word you can expect to hear often in China is *complicated*. Sometimes it is uttered with a resigned sigh, as if to explain why things aren't going as smoothly as you'd like. Other times it is brandished as a veiled warning, meant to imply there is more going on than you could possibly understand, and you'd better not push too hard. Very often it is simply uttered as an excuse.

It's true that things in China are complicated—if it weren't, this chapter would hardly be necessary. But because it is so often true, it also becomes an easy fallback in situations that may not be so complicated after all. On many occasions, I have been told that things are "too complicated" (*tai fuza* in Chinese), and that there is "no way you could comprehend it" (*ni mei fa lijie*), only to think: *It's not so complicated. It's actually quite simple, and I understand it perfectly well: This guy wants more money!*

The "too complicated" gambit presents yet another case where you need to walk a fine line. You do not want to make the mistake of pushing too hard in a situation where it is not appropriate, but neither do you want to forfeit your option to push back at all. It's easy to get hung up on the idea that while in China, you must always yield to Chinese sensibilities. This attitude is easily taken advantage of, and you need to remember that the people in China who are doing business with you are also "stepping out" into unfamiliar turf and should be prepared to make adjustments of their own.

Can You Relate?

Armed with some understanding of what is likely going through the minds of the Chinese people in their interpersonal relationships, you can now begin to think about how you will approach your own various relationships.

Dealing with Employees and Colleagues   When dealing with employees and colleagues, you will be wise to remember that many common Western behaviors tend to rub face-conscious Chinese people the wrong way. That doesn't mean you need to abandon your management style at the customs desk when you get your passport stamped on your way into the country. But you can avoid a lot of problems by being aware of how it is likely to be received, and modulating it to minimize the potential damage.

To protect the face of others, Chinese people tend to leave a lot of obvious things unsaid. They will, for example, be reluctant to call attention to anybody's mistakes or shortcomings. While this saves embarrassment, it means many Chinese organizations do a poor job of analyzing mistakes, learning from them, and preventing recurrences.

In the Chinese medical establishment, then, any hint of a malpractice case tends to be quietly swept under the rug. To pursue it the way the American system typically does—formally reviewing and critiquing decisions made and actions taken—would cause doctors a huge loss of face. As a consequence, the ability to improve systems and procedures is sacrificed.

Any Western manager must therefore strike a balance with Chinese employees. Clearly you do not want to alter your standards or tolerate unacceptable performance from your employees. But if any criticism is carelessly delivered within earshot of others, it will generate huge resentment. When criticism is in order, it should always be delivered in private.

The Therapist Is In...   A lot of Western managers are surprised to find how frequently Chinese employees come to them with personal problems. It can be time-consuming, and it is easy to view it as an unnecessary distraction from work. But investing a little effort into your role as "office therapist" can pay valuable dividends, in terms of both understanding your employees better and earning their trust. On the other hand, a decision to refuse these requests for your time and attention can leave employees thinking you are shirking an important part of your responsibility.

To understand the expectations of these employees, you need to grasp the vital importance of the *danwei,* or "work unit," which under the state-owned enterprise system controlled virtually every aspect of employees' lives. Wherever they worked—whether for a factory, a university, a government ministry, or a company—that institutional affiliation was a big part of their identity. The *danwei* also took responsibility for just about every practical aspect of their life. Housing, medical care, and schooling for their kids were all managed by the *danwei.* Going back farther, so, too, were such personal matters as divorce arbitration and even family planning.

All this resulted in a strong expectation among Chinese workers that their employers would play a role in solving their problems. The *danwei* system is breaking down now, but many people still expect their boss to know and care about their personal problems, and even help solve them. It is not uncommon to spend hours in tearful meetings with employees who come to you with life crises ranging everywhere from their romances to their landlords.

How should you respond? You may not be willing or able to help much, but at a bare minimum you should take enough time to show some level of sympathy and concern. And that can mean resisting your impulse to tell someone to stop bothering you with personal problems and get back to work.

...And So Is the Guidance Counselor Another common challenge for managers lies in getting Chinese employees to exercise independent initiative. Things are, of course, changing as the culture of competitive market economics grows more entrenched. Indeed, the capacity for initiative is already on full display among the many Chinese entrepreneurs who are in business for themselves. But in many cases, you will find that the people working for you (instead of for themselves) are reluctant to take chances, try new things, or make decisions on their own.

The reasons have to do partly with China's education system, which has long stressed rote learning and encouraged conformity. Traditional Chinese bureaucracies have likewise encouraged conformity and discipline, providing high risks and little incentive for anyone stepping out of traditional roles or practices.

This means that if you want your employees to think out of the box and exercise initiative, you will have to provide explicit encouragement and very direct guidance. For many Chinese employees, the default expectation is that they will work according to a well-defined road map, with specific tasks and procedures. If you want them to work according to the more typical Western model—in which employees are given goals and expected to figure out how to meet them—you will have to take the time early on to make those expectations clear, and walk them through.

Dealing with Regulators and Bureaucrats

Among the most important relationships you will have in China are those with the regulators and bureaucrats who, with their power to either grant or deny the countless approvals you need to function, can hold the fate of your business in their hands. In chapter 8, you will read about the problems that can develop when these officials yield to the obvious temptation of corruption.

But even when they do not demand outright bribes, most officials demand respect and acknowledgment of their power. One very important but easily overlooked chore is to keep in touch with these officials on a regular basis. After your initial approvals are in hand, the formal role of some officials may be finished, but that doesn't mean you can stop paying attention to them. They can likely do a great deal to help you if you run into problems later, and it is a very good idea to keep up your friendly ties with an occasional dinner invitation.

In the case of officials who have ongoing involvement in your business, it is likewise a good idea to keep up a steady stream of contact, rather than getting in touch only when there are issues at play. Meeting and entertaining in this way can put your organization on a much friendlier footing for those times when business is an issue.

But this isn't just a matter of deputizing local staff to handle the wining, dining, and occasional gift giving. It is far more effective when senior people from your side are directly involved at least some of the time. If possible, top officials from headquarters should make their way to China themselves every so often, and do so with schedules that are sufficiently flexible to accommodate such courtesy meetings.

When issues are in play, the most important rule is to keep things polite and friendly. Even in an adversarial situation with a regulator, this is vital. You may feel the need to be firm and even push back on official requests, but if you ever lose your cool or become confrontational or aggressive, you will dramatically reduce your odds of a happy ending.

An American manager working in India recently told me about a dispute she was having with a landlord who demanded she not allow guests to visit at certain hours. After extensive discussion, the landlord refused to yield, and the tenant brought it to an end by saying she would have guests come as she pleased, daring the landlord to do something about it.

The ploy seemed to work out well enough for her in India, and the landlord backed down. But my immediate thought was that in China, this strategy would end in absolute disaster. In response to that kind of challenge, a Chinese landlord would be so outraged at the assault on his authority (and yes, his face) that he would undoubtedly feel compelled to indeed "do something about it" to demonstrate his power.

But with a smile, a civil tone, and some patience, you can get your way with regulators. As you've already seen, policies, rules, and laws are often negotiable, and officials usually have a great deal of latitude. The right attitude can do wonders in getting them to lean your way.

Negotiating in China

All these elements of social behavior will be factors in every aspect of your daily life in China, whether around the office or around town. But it is at the negotiating table that it all comes into sharpest relief.

There are many full-length books that cover Chinese negotiating tactics in depth. They range from the sociological theory to the practical application of both political and commercial negotiating techniques. Some of the more worthwhile offerings are listed in the bibliography.

As you are likely to discover early in your China dealings, negotiators are equipped with a full arsenal of heavy-handed techniques aimed at gaining the high ground by unsettling their foreign counterparts. One favorite is the imposition of artificial deadlines to force quick concessions. Another is the introduction of red-herring side issues, or the reopening of issues that were seemingly settled already, in order to prolong negotiations and wear you down. Foreign business people are especially vulnerable to these tactics when they find themselves installed for an extended period at some second-rate hotel in a third-tier Chinese city.

They must also, unfortunately, assume in these situations that their communications are subject to monitoring. While it would be paranoid to assume that everything is monitored all the time, it is always a real possibility, especially in the case of a very high-value deal being negotiated at a high level on the Chinese side. This means it is a good idea to arrive with an established set of parameters and bottom lines, rather than work them out as you go by phone with the home office.

Chinese negotiators will also try to leverage your insecurity about operating in China and your desire to comply with Chinese sensibilities. You can expect to hear the "too complicated" gambit, or that "things are just not done that way" in China.

With all these tactics, patience and composure are the keys to an effective response. Any show of desperation to leave on your part will only lead to added pressure. Anger and firmness may not necessarily be out of place, but will only be productive if kept under control. An outburst reflecting a genuine loss of control or composure is likely to weaken your position.

Maintaining composure is not always easy in the face of outwardly provocative tactics. Stifling feelings of resentment can also be a challenge, as Chinese negotiators seldom show any sign of appreciating the win–win model. There is a shop-worn but nevertheless telling joke among China hands that sums it up nicely: A Chinese chicken was negotiating with a foreign pig to establish a joint venture, and when it came time to decide what to produce, the Chinese chicken proposed—what else?—ham and eggs.

Political Maneuvering

In the United States, Social Security has long been described as the "third rail" of domestic politics: Touch it, and you get zapped. In China, politics itself used to be something of a third rail when it came to social discourse, with equally dangerous consequences for anyone clumsy enough to step on it by mistake. During the endless mass campaigns that raged across China throughout the 1950s, '60s, and '70s, political winds blew hard, and they shifted without warning. The wrong statement, overheard by the wrong ears, could lead to disaster. One of the more harrowing stories I heard during my years in China was from a friend in the southern province of Zhejiang. He spent a decade imprisoned in solitary confinement because, at the height of the political madness of the Cultural Revolution, he was overheard questioning the wisdom of Chairman Mao's pro-growth population policies. It was, of course, only meager consolation for my friend when China totally reversed course after Mao died and instituted its notoriously draconian one-child policy. His tale was hardly unique. Countless others suffered equally harsh fates because of equally innocuous offenses.

By Western standards, Chinese political and civic life today remains oppressive and stultifying. The government is eternally on guard against any attempt by anyone at all to publish unsanctioned views or engage in even the slightest form of political activity that might challenge the Communist party's absolute monopoly on power. Rabble-rousers are dealt with harshly. Long jail sentences are routinely doled out to Internet bloggers, human rights campaigners, or labor activists. In short, any Chinese citizens organizing around any cause at all do so at considerable peril.

Despite all this, it is also fair to say that things have eased in recent years. So long as they steer clear of publishing or formal organizing, people generally feel free to speak their minds on political topics, even in settings where they might be overheard by strangers. Listening in to the conversation at a nearby table in a restaurant, you might well hear bawdy or disparaging jokes about the nation's top leaders. Such jokes are sometimes even sent around by e-mail or text message. You might also hear some heartfelt and fairly bitter grumbling about corruption or unpopular government policies. But everyone in China understands that the freedom to vent about the government over the dinner table is one thing, while even the smallest attempt to challenge it is quite another.

As a foreigner in this environment, it is therefore wise to tread lightly. As you get to know local people, you will have ample chances to talk—or even argue heatedly if you like— about politics. But before reaching that point, you need to make sure the time and the place are right. First meetings are not a good time to try it. A very formal setting, such as a banquet or a large group meeting, is not a good place. And keep in mind that even with people you do know well, and with whom you have developed good personal rapport, discussing politics while their bosses are on hand is likely to lead to the very blandest of answers, and perhaps some awkward silences as well. Not least, it could also cause your counterpart to doubt your trustworthiness and judgment.

In the case of officials who are themselves very senior, you may never find the right time. Officials of higher rank are under considerable pressure to avoid saying things that contravene government policy. And of course, they have a great deal to lose.

Whether you choose to initiate a discussion of politics or simply find yourself thrust into the middle of one, it is vital that you recognize the stakes and sensitivities involved, and understand some of the central issues. You may well have passionate views of your own on some of these issues, and you may very well feel indignant about some of the Chinese government's policies and behaviors. You certainly don't need to abandon your own views, but you'd better make sure you know what's involved if you choose to air them. Above all, you need to know where the red lines and hot buttons lie. Here are some thumbnail reviews of some of the most sensitive issues.

HOT BUTTONS

Topping the list of political hot button issues is, without a doubt, Taiwan. In chapter 8, you will read about some of

the pitfalls that companies can stumble into if they misman-
age this confusing and excruciatingly delicate issue. Meanwhile, in order to avoid problems in your personal dealings
with Chinese counterparts, you should make sure you at least
understand the broad-brush outlines.

Reams have been written about the long-running dispute
over Taiwan. Scholars have made entire careers out of studying the issue, and their work on all the history, the spy-versus-
spy intrigue, the modern day war-gaming, and the painfully
nuanced diplomacy can make for fascinating reading.

In terms of understanding the need-to-know basics, though,
the story is this: The Taiwan problem began in 1949 when the
Nationalist party (Kuomintang in Chinese, or KMT)—which
governed China before and during World War II—was finally
overthrown by Mao Zedong's Communist forces.

With whatever national wealth he could manage to take
with him, KMT leader Chiang Kai-shek fled from the mainland to the island of Taiwan, still claiming to head the rightful government of China, and planning eventually to regroup
and regain control of the entire country. But that was not to
be, and what resulted instead was something of a stalemate.

Mao and the Communists, with considerable Soviet support, founded the People's Republic of China (PRC) and
quickly became too well entrenched for the Nationalists to
have any hope of dislodging them. On Taiwan, meanwhile,
the Nationalist government retained the name Republic
of China (ROC), under which it had previously ruled the
whole country. It also retained recognition from most of the
world as China's legal government, and therefore kept its seat

as one of the Permanent Five members of the UN Security Council.

Perhaps most important of all, Taiwan retained the support and protection of the United States, which was enough to deter the mainland from trying to take Taiwan. Though it didn't move militarily, the PRC all along insisted Taiwan was an "inalienable" part of its territory that it temporarily happened not to control. And Beijing steadfastly declined to have any formal dealings with any other nation that refused to acknowledge the point.

By the early 1970s, many Western nations, the United States included, understood that they needed to develop ties with mainland China, even though it would mean dropping formal recognition of Taiwan. By the end of the decade, Taiwan had lost its seat in the United Nations and the diplomatic recognition of most of the world's major countries.

Since then, Taiwan has developed a flourishing trade-based economy and a lively democratic political culture, but remains shut out of international institutions. China does huge amounts of business with the island, and hundreds of thousands of Taiwanese live and work in China. But the mainland still insists it is part of its territory, and promises to use force if necessary to keep it from declaring formal independence. The big wild card in that case would be the response of the United States, which could choose to intervene to protect Taiwan from a mainland attack, or stand by and let events proceed. In an effort to deter dangerous adventurism from either side, the US government maintains a policy of "strategic ambiguity" about how it might actually respond.

A vocal but small minority of Taiwanese do advocate steps toward independence, and another small minority would like to see the two sides reunify on or close to mainland terms. The majority, though, favor keeping the status quo, in which Taiwan manages its own affairs and continues to prosper as if it were a country—but refrains from provoking China by saying so outright.

Opinion on the mainland side is much less diverse. With very few exceptions, people support the official line—namely, that China's sovereignty over Taiwan is a sacred point of national honor, that anything to do with Taiwan is strictly a matter of China's "internal affairs," and that the United States commits a grave offense whenever it sells arms to Taiwan or hints at the possibility of defending it against a potential mainland attack.

The key point for you to understand is that, from the mainland point of view, it is utter heresy to refer to Taiwan as "independent" or as a "country." In the right situation, you may wish to talk openly in China about your thoughts on the matter, but you need to be aware of the passionate response you are likely to generate.

Tibet

Another very sensitive topic is China's relationship with Tibet. The government line on Tibet is that the vast and mountainous Buddhist region has been part of China for centuries, and that since 1959, when its army moved in and the Dalai Lama fled to India, China has ruled it benevolently, lavishing vast amounts of money on building up the region's infrastructure and raising the living standards of the Tibetan people.

China's claim of age-old sovereignty is widely disputed by Western scholars, and there is no doubt that China's current rule has been oppressive, especially when it comes to religious practice in the region. Although the Dalai Lama insists he seeks genuine autonomy for Tibetans rather than independence, China considers him a "splittist" masquerading as a religious leader who is bent on breaking up the motherland. Again, opinion within China is virtually unanimous in support of the official line, and many Chinese are puzzled by the rock-star status and cult following the Dalai Lama has garnered in the West.

Japan, Human Rights, Chairman Mao, and Tiananmen Square

There are a handful of other touchy political issues that need to be handled carefully. One is China's troubled relationship with Japan. Most Chinese remain full of resentment over Japan's brutal occupation of China before and during World War II, and its failure in the years since to come to terms with its past. As with Taiwan, China's economic relationship with Japan is vast, vibrant, and vital. But in their hearts, many—if not most—Chinese people actively resent and dislike Japan. On several occasions in recent years, these feelings have been vented in violent demonstrations again Japanese businesses, interests, and people in China. Though China remains an important market and manufacturing base for Japanese

companies, many Japanese executives feel increasingly uncomfortable living in China.

The Tiananmen Square demonstrations of 1989, and their
violent suppression by the Chinese army, is another touchy
issue. Hundreds were killed in the streets of Beijing, and a brutal crackdown continued for months afterward. In Chinese
parlance, the incident is referred to as June 4 (*liu si,* in Chinese,
meaning "6/4"), for the date the deadly assault occurred. Privately, many Chinese—especially residents of Beijing who are
old enough to remember it—remain repulsed by what the government did, but you must remember that in formal or public
situations, they will not feel comfortable talking about it.

When it comes to human rights more generally, many Chinese people have a clear understanding of the shortcomings
in their system. But they are also sensitive about the tendency
of outsiders to comment or criticize. And they are downright
puzzled by the way the US and other Western governments feel
compelled to make an issue of yet another Chinese "internal
affair." It is another area where you need to tread carefully.

Lastly, there is the question of Chairman Mao. Gone are the
days when he was worshipped as a near god, but he remains
widely revered—even though he himself would be shocked at
how enthusiastically China has embraced capitalism.

To deal with the obvious excesses of his reign, China after
his death in 1976 adopted an official line stating that his
actions were 70 percent correct and 30 percent wrong. Even
with that, few Chinese care to dwell on the bad side. Jokes
about him are not likely to be well received, and negative
comments should not be made in public settings. Made in

private, they will launch you on yet one more interesting discussion. Make them if you care to, but as with all these issues, you should at least understand what you are getting into.

THE LITTLE THINGS

Now that you have an understanding of the Big Stuff—including face, *guanxi,* and politics—and the Small Stuff, like the etiquette surrounding banquet behavior, gift giving, and common manners, it is time to consider yet another category, which I call the Little Things.

These are the countless things that a foreign business person might never think twice about but that could leave locals fuming. One simple example: Skipping meals is just about unheard of in China, so asking anyone—be it an office assistant, an official, or a roomful of dignitaries attending a seminar—to "work through lunch" will earn you nothing but scorn.

Punctuality is similarly important. Traffic in Beijing, Shanghai, and many other cities is absolutely atrocious, and it can be easy to run seriously late for meetings or appointments. But to do so, especially for any formal function, is considered very bad form, and despite the traffic you will find that most Chinese people manage to arrive on time. You should, too. Many Chinese, especially older people or senior officials, will be more than slightly insulted to be left waiting for you at a formal function.

You should also keep track of the Chinese lunar calendar and its many holidays. China takes a full week off for three major holidays: the May 1 Labor Day, the October 1 National Day, and the lunar new year, also called the Spring Festival, which can fall anywhere during January or February. In addition, there are other meaningful holidays, such as the midautumn festival when families traditionally eat together under the full moon, and the April 5 Qing Ming holiday, when people are supposed to visit cemeteries and sweep clean the graves of their ancestors.

It is clearly not possible for a Western company to schedule time off for these and other Chinese holidays, but you should be aware how meaningful it is for Chinese people to spend time with their families on these occasions. What you *can* do is pay attention to the Chinese lunar calendar, know when the holidays fall, and wherever possible, avoid scheduling big events or asking employees to travel or work late on those days. If conflicts are unavoidable, you should at least make sure to let people know that you are aware of the sacrifice you are asking them to make and that you appreciate it. Imposing on them this way will sometimes prove unavoidable. But doing so without even acknowledging it will leave many people with a sour taste—and the impression that you do not understand or respect the culture you've chosen to work in.

MY FRIEND MICHAEL

By now you have some understanding of Chinese behavior and etiquette on matters large and small. But it is important to keep things in perspective.

There is, of course, plenty of value to be had in mastering the intricacies of Chinese culture and manners. Among the Western business community in China, there are many accomplished China hands—the sort of people who speak perfect Chinese, know every last point of etiquette, and can with equal ease sing modern Chinese pop tunes or recite ancient proverbs and Tang dynasty poetry while at the same time dazzling you with their calligraphy technique. Without a doubt, their skills in these areas are impressive and do much to enhance their ability to make friends and influence people in China.

But at the end of the day, your success or failure in China will depend a lot more on the basic fundamentals of your business. It will depend on the vital choices you make about how to structure your venture, and on your skill in choosing the right partners. And most of all—just like anywhere else in the world—it will depend on the merits of your product, your efficiency in managing costs, and your ability to deliver value.

To illustrate this point, I'd like to introduce you to my good friend Michael Komesaroff. He stands in sharp contrast with the classical Western China hand. Michael is an Australian consultant specializing in China's capital-intensive industries, and you would be hard-pressed to find anyone more knowledgeable about China's mining, power, transport, or metal industries. He lived in China for a couple of years during the 1990s and continues to visit frequently on business. But when it comes to the traditional dos and don'ts of Chinese business etiquette, he's not exactly a poster child. He doesn't much bother with formalities. He dresses for comfort. He is hard-driving, direct, and sometimes downright raucous, especially with his humor. He is more likely to reel off an outrageous joke than a profound ancient proverb. Despite his years of living and working in China, he hasn't learned a word of the language. In fact, he can barely pronounce the names of the people he meets and the places he visits. On top of it all, he happens not to like Chinese food very much. He'll eat it if he must, and without complaint, but given his choice he'd much rather have something else.

Yet he is highly successful. How does he do it? The answers are simple. He is sincere. He deals straight and treats people well, gaining their trust and access to the information he depends on to run his business. Despite his forthright manner, his respect for people shows through. Whatever he lacks in his understanding of Chinese culture, he makes up for with basic common sense. Not least, he knows his business, and he delivers what he promises.

It is a simple formula, and one that can be as effective in China as anywhere else in the world.

KEY POINTS TO REMEMBER
FROM CHAPTER 3

1. For foreign women in business, gender is often less of an issue in China than it is at home. The fact that they are foreign will blot out everything else in the eyes of many of the Chinese people they deal with.
2. Chinese etiquette falls into two categories: the Big Stuff that you can't afford to ignore, and the Small

Stuff that is nice to know but less than crucial. As a foreigner, you aren't necessarily expected to understand the Small Stuff, and you will be granted considerable leeway for any lapses. Indeed, against these lowered expectations, you can easily score valuable points when you do get things right. But screwing up on the Big Stuff can cause you Big Problems.

3. Understand the concepts of face and *guanxi*. They are subtle and hard to grasp, but they are often front and center in the thinking of the Chinese people you deal with.

4. Norms of communication are different in China. People are reluctant to say no, even when no is what they mean. Chinese people will not likely volunteer any information you didn't ask for specifically, and if you ever think, *They would have told me if that was the case!*—you are almost certainly wrong.

5. When dealing with employees, criticism delivered within earshot of others will generate huge resentment. If criticism is in order, it should be delivered in private.

6. To get Chinese employees to think outside the box and exercise initiative, you will often need to provide explicit encouragement and very direct guidance. For many Chinese employees, the default expectation is that they will work according to a well-defined road map.

7. Don't forget to maintain your relationships with officials, even when you have no business pending with

them. It can become awkward to approach them only when you need something, so keep the channels open during slow periods. And make sure that senior people in your organization invest some of their own time in these relationships.

8. Maintain composure in negotiations. Many Chinese negotiating tactics are specifically intended to make you lose your cool, and you will damage your position if you do. Patience is key. Anger and firmness have their place, but only if used in a controlled way.

9. Politics remains a touchy subject in China. On issues such as Taiwan, Tibet, and human rights, the government—and most individuals—have very strong views. Understand the issues before you risk talking about them, and choose the situations carefully. You can embarrass people and possibly even get them into serious trouble by talking about politics in the wrong way at the wrong time.

10. Apart from the Big Stuff and the Small Stuff are the Little Things: actions you might not think twice about but that can leave Chinese people fuming. Learn what they are and keep them in mind.

11. Maintain perspective! Etiquette is important, sometimes vitally so. But you will not get by on etiquette alone. At the end of the day, your success will depend on your business fundamentals, and your company's ability to deliver.

4

⟨⟩

Sales and Marketing

Having read this far, you already know a fair bit about the Chinese business landscape—its hottest sectors, its complex legal environment, and its bafflingly unique social and commercial culture. So it should come as no great surprise to learn that when you get down to the nuts and bolts of selling and marketing in China, some of the most basic maxims of doing business simply do not apply.

Whether it's the theories that you learned in business school or the tactics and strategies that have served you so well in other markets, you will need to adapt—and in some cases discard—a lot of what you know once you get to China.

To name just a few examples, the value of branding, the role of advertising, and the importance of quality in the marketplace all operate differently in China. (For proof, you need only consider the ready willingness of so many Chinese consumers to knowingly purchase knockoff products and substandard no-name goods.) To mount a successful marketing effort in China, you will need to take such differences into account when you design your strategy.

Meanwhile, to execute your strategy—whether your goal is to sell consumer goods to millions of ordinary Chinese or to win hefty procurement contracts on big-ticket capital equipment items from government procurers—you will have to factor in China's unique logistical challenges. On both the hardware and the software sides, the nation's business-support infrastructure is often lacking. From banking to distribution logistics, many of the basic facilities and services that you might take for granted in more developed markets cannot be relied upon in China.

For one simple example, imagine your business involves perishable products—say, frozen foods. You will have to plan on devoting a lot of time, effort, and money to ensuring reliable cold-storage transport for those goods. In the best case, you will need to commit staff and resources *on an ongoing basis* to the job of supervising and managing every link in your shipping process to make sure your goods are not being repeatedly thawed and refrozen along the way.

In the worst case, you may have to spend even more time and money developing an adequate shipping process yourself, from the ground up.

But in no case will you be able to count on finding an adequate, ready-made solution that will smoothly run for a prolonged period on autopilot. Despite the glitz and glamour of the modern cities where your operation is likely to be headquartered, China remains a developing country where nothing much *ever* runs for long on autopilot. Any business plan that fails to budget for this fact of life is bound to lead to disappointment.

At the same time, though, it would be a mistake to assume that *everything* in China is incomprehensibly different or unique. This will be especially clear to anyone who has had previous experience working in other developing markets. These people will find many of China's challenges all too familiar. Most foreigners upon arrival in China are quick to understand that they are not in Kansas anymore. But that does not mean they have landed in some kind of Oz where the laws of Newtonian physics somehow fail to hold sway.

However great China's cultural, political, and developmental differences may be, some basic business principles *do* remain the same. If, for example, you are assuming you've got it made in China on the strength of your terrific *guanxi* alone, you would do well to remember that here, just like anywhere else, performance and value still matter at the end of the day. In a similar vein, the laws of supply and demand still apply in China—even if market and information distortions do sometimes conspire to camouflage that fact.

You will therefore do yourself no favor if you totally abandon your standard marketing tool kit when you get to China. The real trick lies in knowing which tools are likely to work, which ones are not, and which ones need to be modified. The task is made all the more difficult by the fact that China, in addition to being so different in so many ways, is changing all the time.

KEEPING IT LEGAL

As you contemplate your broader approach to reaching, wooing, and keeping all your potential Chinese customers, you will need to think strategically about how you set things up. As with just about everything else, the laws governing the ways foreign companies may sell in China vary widely from place to place, and from product to product. These laws also change frequently; fortunately, most of those changes are trending toward greater flexibility and liberalization. This chapter can sketch the outlines of it all for you, but in order to be sure of properly structuring an operation, you will need specialized legal professionals to help you tackle the specifics.

In most jurisdictions in China, permits to sell and permits to import are granted separately. So after dealing with officials from the customs, product safety, and foreign exchange bureaucracies to obtain import permission, a foreign company that wants to handle its own sales and distribution would then have to approach another set of commerce, tax, and other regulators for yet more permits.

Sales and distribution rights, in turn, are usually granted separately for retail and wholesale operations. At the end of 2004, as more of its WTO obligations kicked in, China began allowing foreign investors to take 100 percent equity positions in many types of retailing and wholesaling ventures. But certain equity caps can still apply, based on either product categories or the size of an operation. Foreign retailers with thirty or more outlets, for example, have been limited to minority holdings.

Such restrictions continue to get phased out all the time. In December, 2006, five years after China's accession, another round of WTO-mandated liberalizations took effect and restrictions were lifted on products ranging from cars to chemical fertilizers.

Despite these and other central government moves, there are officials in many provinces who still get away with enforcing their own geographic restrictions on sales operations— requiring, for example, that foreign firms limit their operations to provincial capital cities or officially designated "special economic zones." Depending on what you are trying to sell, these restrictions may not in the end be so onerous, because the spending power and market potential beyond these cities and zones often remains unappealing. And it is a fair bet that by the time such places do become attractive, rules and regulations will have been further relaxed.

BARRIERS TO SUCCESS?

Apart from these legal and regulatory hassles—which are always time-consuming, often frustrating, but usually surmountable— what are the other obstacles to selling your products in China?

If you were to judge from some of the ranting that regularly emanates from the US Congress, you might well conclude that the Chinese market is an impenetrable fortress of protectionism. The rhetoric, reminiscent of the accusations made against Japan in the 1980s, tends to run hottest around election time and usually includes calls for "open markets" and "a level playing field." Ominously, it is also often accompanied by threats to enact trade sanctions or other retaliatory measures against China.

Fueling the uproar is China's consistently huge trade surplus with the United States, which according to US Customs statistics totaled a staggering $202 billion for 2005.

One of the main charges made by critics is that China manipulates its currency, keeping the yuan artificially low in order to make Chinese exports cheaper and imported goods more expensive.

There is no doubt that China does indeed manage its currency. Wary of any potential instability in its financial system, and especially nervous about potential exposure to the kind of rampant currency speculation that helped trigger the 1997 Asian financial crisis, the Chinese government maintains strict capital account controls, and it continues to resist calls to make the yuan fully convertible. For current account transactions, it allows the yuan exchange rate to fluctuate only within a very narrow band.

There aren't many mainstream economists who would deny that the yuan is in fact undervalued. Opinions vary as to just how undervalued it is, and estimates among credible analysts tend to fall within the 15 to 25 percent range. But economists are likewise united in thinking that, congressional election-year rhetoric notwithstanding, the exchange rate plays only a tiny role in the huge trade deficit America runs with China.

The true cause of the deficit is a complex set of structural factors on both sides. The most obvious is the mirror-image phenomenon that sees the United States consistently spending more than it earns, buying on credit, and saving hardly anything, while China does the opposite: saving voraciously and resisting the government's efforts to encourage citizens to generate some economic stimulus by spending more.

Yet another factor is China's emergence as an Asian processing hub. Since the 1990s, manufacturers of all kinds from Taiwan, South Korea, Japan, and elsewhere have moved big chunks of their assembly and production operations to China. Designs, brand names, and components still come from those countries, but when the goods are finished and shipped to the United States, they end up counting as imports from China. The clearest illustration of this dynamic is the fact that China's rising surplus with the United States has been neatly matched in recent years by an offsetting decline in the US trade balance with the rest of Asia.

If Chinese currency manipulation isn't to blame for the trade imbalance, what is? After all, isn't our $202 billion bilateral trade deficit proof enough that somehow China is unfairly protecting its markets? The surprising answer is: "Not really."

According to economist Nicholas Lardy, a senior fellow at the Institute for International Economics in Washington and one of the world's top China specialists, China is no doubt guilty of trying to protect certain industries and product groups, sometimes even violating its WTO commitments to do so. "But," Lardy has testified before Congress, "China is certainly one of the most open—perhaps the most open—of all emerging market economies."

He cited Chinese import volumes, which have recorded staggering increases since the early 1990s, growing even faster than China's much-ballyhooed GDP growth rate. China's import ratio (the proportion of imported goods compared with total GDP) has risen dramatically, typically running four times higher than Japan's and twice as high as that of the United States.

When it comes to import tariffs, China also scores well for openness. According to Lardy, China's average import tariff rate peaked at 55 percent in 1982. It had already been reduced to 15 percent by 2001 when China joined the WTO, and it has fallen to less than 10 percent since then. Meanwhile, average import tariffs in places such as Brazil, Argentina, India, and Indonesia range from three to four times higher.

Perhaps the most convincing indicator of China's relative openness is the fact that it actually runs a pretty big deficit with the rest of the world. In general, China either has balanced trade or enjoys modest surpluses with most European Union countries, and it tends to run large deficits with other Asian nations.

For 2005, China reported an overall trade surplus of $101 billion. That sounds healthy indeed, but remember that its surplus with the United States alone stood at $202 billion. Factoring out that single anomalous trade relationship, China in 2005 bought *$101 billion more* in imports than it sold in exports. Clearly, then, many foreign firms *are* finding ways to sell into China.

CHINESE CONSUMERS

If all this proves that selling into the China market is possible, it doesn't mean it's easy. An important first step is to gain an understanding of who China's consumers are and what they want. And that's not easy, either, because when you take this challenge on, you are aiming at a target that never stands still.

Nowhere is China's fast-changing nature more apparent than in its consumer culture. Indeed, the very concept of a consumer culture is itself a relative novelty in modern China. For the first three decades after the 1949 Communist take-over, China was more like a consumer wasteland.

For years, the conventional wisdom maintained that China at its core was simply not a materialistic society. This was easy for many Westerners to buy into because it fit so well with some of the common (and overly romantic) notions they held about China. It also went down well on the Chinese side, because virtues such as austerity and selflessness were a perfect fit with the government's political narrative and China's self-proclaimed identity as a developing socialist country.

But guess what. It really wasn't true. What I began to suspect way back in my earliest days in China has since been confirmed many times over: Chinese society was not at all lacking in the natural human tendency toward materialism. What it lacked at the time was any "material" to pursue.

Few consumers had much discretionary spending power and, under the nation's strict central planning regime, few producers had to worry about satisfying them. Products were manufactured to low standards, packaged unattractively, and advertised hardly at all. A handful of well-known brand names existed all along, but they were certainly not cultivated or leveraged in any sense that Western marketers would recognize.

If you lived in China in those days and wanted to buy something—be it shoes, shampoo, or soy sauce—you went to a dreary state-run store. You dealt with the surly clerk, and you took whatever they had. Or not. Neither the store nor the manufacturer had much of anything riding on your decision.

The factories were told what and how much to make by state planning officials, and the stores were told what to sell at what prices. If at the end of the planning period, their books failed to add up, they would simply be subsidized by so-called loans from state-owned banks.

Managers were under no pressure to make profits or to outperform their competitors, and they usually didn't have to worry about repaying those loans, either. Their biggest headache was meeting their obligation to provide housing, education, pensions, and health care for their workers and dependent families. From the government's point of view, it was worthwhile to keep loaning them money that would never be paid back, so long as they kept their people in line by meeting those basic needs.

All this began to change when market-oriented reforms were launched in the late 1970s, and at first things changed only slowly. By 1989, when I got to China, private entrepreneurs had begun to emerge, but they remained a besieged minority class with a reputation as somewhat untrustworthy mavericks.

Meanwhile, television commercials still reflected an economy that had yet to venture too far from the central planning model. Ads for penny-ante consumer goods such as dishwashing soap and instant noodles had already started to appear on Chinese television, but they were interspersed with delightfully bizarre commercials for things like construction equipment and water treatment systems.

Television advertising may have seemed like an inefficient and scattershot way to reach the relatively tiny number of enterprise managers or government officials with the power to make buying decisions like that, but it makes more sense when you consider that such people were just about the only viewers with any substantial spending power at all.

Things are dramatically different today. In giving freer range to private entrepreneurs, China has created whole new classes of wealthy and middle-class people, and they have taken quickly to the consumer lifestyle. Other reforms have even transferred modest amounts of buying power into the hands of people who have yet to break through to middle-class status.

Under China's old *danwei* or "work unit" system, described in chapter 3, most people had their basic needs met through their employer. Housing, schooling, medical care, and even basic food rations were all chosen and procured by the work unit, and monetary salaries were tiny. As reforms began to dismantle that system, individuals got more of their compensation in cash, and made more of their own decisions about where to spend it. And all of a sudden producers and retailers had a stake in getting their attention. The single most significant of those reforms involved housing.

At the Car Wash with Larry Summers and Zhu Rongji

It was former US Treasury Secretary Lawrence Summers who famously said that "no one in the history of the world ever washed a rented car." His appreciation of the natural link between ownership of an asset and the incentive to invest in it was shared by Zhu Rongji, the popular, no-nonsense former mayor of Shanghai who became China's prime minister in 1998. Zhu and Summers ended up spending quite a bit of time together and got along well, despite the fact that many of their meetings dealt with very prickly trade disputes. Zhu, with something much like Summers's car wash logic in mind, believed that housing reform could, in a single stroke, solve several of the biggest problems plaguing China's economy.

One of those problems was labor mobility. Workers' homes were tied to their jobs, and larger, nicer apartments were usually awarded according to seniority. So even after reforms gave people unprecedented latitude to live and work where they chose, they were reluctant to take advantage of it if it meant they would lose their housing. The more senior and the more accomplished people were, the more they had to lose. In Zhu's eyes, this obstacle to the movement of talent undermined the efficiency of the labor market and caused unnecessary drag on Chinese productivity. Breaking that link between jobs and homes was one key objective of the housing reforms.

Even more importantly, Zhu recognized the stimulus potential that could be unlocked if one of China's biggest assets—the entire nationwide stock of residential real estate—were to be suddenly monetized. As a knock-on effect, people who owned their own homes might well become willing to invest in them, spending huge sums on the sort of maintenance, decoration, and improvements that they previously had no incentive to pay for. At long last, they would "wash their cars."

Today the easiest way to see the results is to make a quick visit to Beijing's Ikea superstore or any of the nation's thousands of other furniture and home improvement stores. There you will find people who ten and fifteen years ago couldn't be bothered to change a lightbulb or sweep the floor in the common stairwell of their *danwei* housing but are now enthusiastically spending big sums to fix up the homes they own.

The Chinese government has been doing everything it can to encourage consumer spending in other areas, too. It is well aware that the Chinese growth miracle has relied too heavily on export markets abroad and fixed asset investment at home, and it knows that the key to sustaining future growth lies with domestic demand. That means getting Chinese consumers to save less and spend more, and millions of them have taken to it like fish to water.

Chinese Consumers—Who Are They?

By now, of course, most Western business people already know better than to assume that every one of China's 1.3 billion citizens is a potential customer. It was the Western dreamers of centuries past who fantasized about getting rich by selling just a tiny bit of something—anything—to everyone in China.

Today's dreamers tend to work the fantasy somewhat differently, imagining that if they can gain a foothold now in this growing market, China's steadily rising standard of living will generate a constant stream of new middle-class customers. And they are probably right. That 1.3-billion-strong Holy Grail will long remain out of reach, but there is no shortage of credible projections suggesting that tens upon tens of millions of potential customers will be moving within range in the near-term future.

But what about the situation right now? China's Academy of Social Sciences defines *middle-class people* as those who usually have a college education and work in white-collar jobs. They have individual earnings of between 25,000 and 30,000 yuan ($3,125 to $3,750) per year, and annual household purchasing power that is three times higher. It is estimated that somewhere around fifty million Chinese households already qualify as middle class by these standards, and more are joining the club at a steady clip. By 2010, the number is expected to rise to between 100 and 120 million households.

In a more detailed breakdown, analysts at the securities firm BNP Paribas Peregrine have divided Chinese consumers into six separate categories (see table 4.1). At the bottom are the sixty million subsistence-level households that get by on individual incomes of less than $300 per year and hardly register as viable consumers.

At the top are an estimated six million luxury-consuming households whose members earn $6,000 per year or more and are already spending money on items such as cars, second homes, foreign vacations, designer fashions, and golf.

TABLE 4.1

OVERVIEW OF CHINA'S CONSUMPTION STRUCTURE

Consumer Category	Total Number (in millions of households)	Percentage of Total Population (%)	Per Capita Income ($/year)	General Classification Criterion	What They Buy	Where They Buy
Luxury Consumers	6.0	1.6	Above 6,000	They own cars	Top global brands	High-end department stores or overseas shopping
Brand Consumers	46.1	12.3	3,000–6,000	They own computers	National brands, low to middle global brands	Department stores or exclusive stores
Quality-Sensitive Consumers	70.2	18.7	1,500–3,000	They own air conditioners	Middle brands	Grocery chain stores
Price-Sensitive Consumers	73.8	19.7	800–1,500	They own refrigerators	Local brands	Cheap grocery stores
Staple Consumers	118.4	31.6	300–800	They own TV sets	Nonbrands or cheap staples	Open bazaars or wet markets
Subsistence Living	60.4	16.1	Below 300	They do not own TV sets	Nonbrands	Self-supplied or open bazaars

SOURCE: Courtesy of Erwin Sanft and Raymond Ma of BNP Paribas Peregrine. Used by permission.

In between, the other categories include staple consumers who probably own a TV but not a refrigerator and are just one major illness away from falling to subsistence level; and price-sensitive consumers who do own a refrigerator and will shop to fill it, but need to shop carefully to make their money last.

Further up are the quality-sensitive consumers who have yet to hit it big but who do have enough spare income to travel for leisure within China, buy and run an air conditioner, and keep up a bank balance at the same time; above them are the brand consumers who typically buy international and top-tier domestic-brand products, already own a computer, and are probably thinking about getting a car sometime soon.

Apart from the distinctions outlined in this matrix, there are two other crucial variables that determine consumer attitudes and behavior. One is the urban–rural divide; the other, the generation gap. While generalizations are always risky, it is fair to say that older Chinese, together with rural dwellers, are far more conservative in their attitudes. Both groups are far more reluctant to borrow for consumption purposes, and they are far more resistant to new ideas and new product categories, including foreign brands.

In the case of the urban–rural divide, there is a great deal of overlap with the other categories. Almost all subsistence-level consumers and about five out of six staple consumers live in rural areas.

Above those levels, the ratios shift. Two out of three price-sensitive consumers are urban. For the quality-sensitive consumers at the next level up, that ratio is seven out of eight.

At the highest levels, among brand and luxury consumers, the vast majority are urban.

The picture is more complex when it comes to the generational divide. Regardless of whether they live in the cities or the rural areas, and whatever their income, China's young people are forging a distinctive identity and developing bolder attitudes.

It should not be at all surprising, considering how very different their experiences have been. Just about anyone born in a large city after the 1979 implementation of the family-planning policy was an only child. Even in the countryside, where families often manage to have two children, family sizes have become far smaller than they used to be. In either case, these kids were raised with a lot more attention paid to their desires, and at most just one other sibling to compete with. The result has been a generation of what Chinese people often call "Little Emperors."

Sociologists have long worried about what the emergence of this cohort will do to Chinese society and its standards of civility and ethics. But for marketers it is a dream come true: a whole generation of people who are growing increasingly wealthy, and who are used to getting what they want.

Chinese Consumers—What *Do* They Want?

So what is it these eager young consumers want? The general answer is "just about everything." But when it comes to specifics, the answers can sometimes be surprising.

It was long believed, for example, that Chinese consumers would never take to dairy products. Milk was never a big part of the diet, and cheese was an exotic foreign food hardly known in China. Indeed, many Chinese are lactose-intolerant and have trouble digesting any kind of milk products. Ice cream, went the wisdom, was doubly doomed to fail because of the widespread Chinese aversion to very cold foods, based on the principles of Chinese medicine.

In fact, things have turned out differently. Giant multinationals such as Nestlé, Danone, and Unilever are competing with hundreds of Chinese companies to meet China's skyrocketing demand for milk, yogurt, and, yes, ice cream. The Dairy Association of China expects to see annual nationwide milk consumption rise from the 2005 level of 21.7 kilograms per person to 40 kilograms by 2020.

Pizza Hut and Papa John's, among others, are meanwhile doing big business selling their melted cheese offerings all over China. When parent company Yum! Brands, Inc., opened its first Pizza Hut in Beijing in 1990, it started off as an expatriate hangout. Today the company has two hundred stores across the country. In its first fifteen years in China, the Pizza Hut division has sold fifty million pizzas and racked up nearly $700 million in total sales. Having established itself in all of China's top-tier cities, Pizza Hut is now pushing into second-tier locations.

Domestic imitators have hopped on the bandwagon, too. In such far-flung locations as Kunming, in southwestern Yunnan Province, and Baotou, in Inner Mongolia, I have been surprised to see local restaurants offering pizza. Their own variations on the fine art of pizza making might make connoisseurs in New York or Chicago cringe, but their existence is ample testimony to the fact that a lot of conventional wisdom in today's changing China deserves a rethink.

Still, it cannot be assumed that Chinese tastes will always tend toward convergence with Western ones. Consider, for example, the different factors that go into a Chinese car buyer's decision-making process. Besides quality and low prices, what is it that Chinese car buyers are looking for, and how do their preferences differ from those of consumers in other markets?

For one thing, since they have not grown up around cars the way most Americans have, Chinese buyers tend not to know much about what's under the hood. They are less interested in hearing about all those robust performance specs at the heart of so much car marketing in the United States. Instead, they want to hear about safety, reliability, and cost. So passenger air bags are of more concern than rack-and-pinion steering, and fuel economy is a far better selling point than fuel injection.

After all, unlike America where so many car owners live in the suburbs, Chinese car owners live mainly in the nation's traffic-plagued cities. Why should it matter to them how long it takes to go from zero to sixty? For the most part, it simply doesn't.

Chinese car buyers do pay close attention to the status value of the cars they choose. But again, the *way* they pay attention is different. Private vehicles are still new enough in China that car ownership is something of a status symbol in itself. So even those buyers who are stretching their finances to get themselves behind the wheel of a budget-class model are still hoping to make a statement. That's why interior bells and whistles, whether plush or faux plush, are such big attractions on even the smallest and most humble models.

In a book like this, such examples of consumer attitudes are useful as a way to convey a sense of what factors are at play in the China market. Of course, the people for whom these attitudes really matter most—the world's top carmakers—are tracking trends and preferences in excruciating detail, scrambling to adapt their vehicles as if their very futures depended on it. Which in fact they might.

SUITING LOCAL TASTES AND HABITS

Up and down the line, from carmakers to fast-food vendors, foreign companies have found the need to adapt their products to local tastes. KFC, another Yum! Brands chain, is wildly popular in China. In fact, Harland Sanders, aka the Colonel, was named by the *People's Daily* in 2006 as one of the fifty foreigners who have had the greatest influence on China since 1840! But clearly, the influence stream has run in both directions. KFC has experimented with all sorts of menu items specially designed to appeal to Chinese tastes. These have included a spinach-and-egg soup, a rice porridge offering, and the "Old Beijing Twister," a chicken item dressed with spring onions and hoisin sauce and served in the style of a traditional Peking duck pancake wrap.

It is also important to recognize the differences in Chinese buying habits. For example, despite rising living standards and the housing reforms of recent years, many Chinese continue to live in dwellings that are small by American standards. However new and gleaming their kitchens may be, few people opt for the typical American double-wide refrigerator. And few have garages, basements, or other storage areas.

In addition, the traditional practice of shopping each day for fresh food remains very much entrenched. Finally, car owners remain a minority in China, so more shoppers are using public transport or walking home with their groceries rather than tossing them in the trunk of a car. Add this all up, and the obvious conclusion is that standard American bulk packaging, either of foods or household supplies, is not a good choice for the China market.

KEY POINTS TO REMEMBER
FROM CHAPTER 4

1. When you get to China, you are definitely not in Kansas anymore—but that doesn't mean you're in Oz. Some of the marketing tools you bring with you will work, but they'll also need to be adapted.

2. You will need to jump through some bureaucratic hoops before you start selling your products in China. Permission to import and permission to sell are granted separately. Retail and wholesale distribution

are also governed separately. Local governments may complicate your life further with rules of their own.

3. There are plenty of maddening obstacles on the path to setting up and selling in China. It is not for the fainthearted. But China is *not* the protectionist fortress that Congress and US industry groups like to claim it is. Its currency is somewhat undervalued, but this plays only a tiny role in the American trade deficit with China. Its tariff barriers are far below those of many other countries, and its import ratio is very high. Factoring out its anomalous trade relationship with the United States, China actually buys far more from the rest of the world than it sells.

4. Consumer culture is relatively new to China, but it sure has caught on. People like to buy things, and the government—eager to rebalance the economy with less weight on export-led growth and fixed asset investment—is doing everything it can to encourage them.

5. Chinese consumers can only be classified according to a complex matrix, taking into account generational differences, the urban–rural divide, and their vastly diverse income levels. All must be targeted appropriately, and the targets seldom stand still. There is constant movement among the categories as rural dwellers head to the cities and as rising incomes carry people farther up the consumption chart.

6. Be wary of stereotypes and clichés about what Chinese consumers may or may not like. Conventional

wisdom long maintained that dairy products such as ice cream or cheese would never sell in China, but brands like Pizza Hut would beg to differ—and they have the revenue from the fifty million pizzas they've already sold to prove their point.

7. Understand local tastes and buying habits and tailor your offerings to meet them. Everything from packaging to brand positioning needs to take Chinese differences into account. For example, since car ownership in itself is a huge status symbol in China, buyers of even the humblest models can be psychologically invested in the status statement that their vehicles make.

5

Information, Please!

The information landscape in China is one of those areas where you can choose to view the glass as either half empty or half full. Recent years have seen undeniably vast progress in the volume and timeliness of the information that is available, both from official sources within China and from outside analysts about China. All that progress notwithstanding, there remain huge shortcomings in the quality, accuracy, and reliability of what information is available. And above all, there remains an ingrained bureaucratic tendency toward secrecy.

While that tendency exists to some extent in all governments and all systems, it is especially prominent in China where it is reinforced by cultural norms and thousands of years of official practice. The difficulties are compounded by the nation's lack of independent sources of alternative information. In this environment, finding the information you need—and can trust—will be one of your biggest challenges.

Despite the substantial obstacles, though, it is possible for foreign business people to find out what they need to know— or most of it, anyway. This chapter will not only tell you how and where to find information vital to your understanding of China and the operation of your business, but also how to *evaluate* that information.

HUGE FLOOD, NO INFORMATION

First, to get a sense of how much things have changed already, consider what happened in the central Chinese province of Henan in the predawn hours of August 8, 1975. Following several days of abnormally heavy rains that had swelled the human-made Banqiao Reservoir, local villagers were frantically working to reinforce an eighty-foot-tall dam on the Huai River. In an instant, though, the dam—built in the 1950s according to shoddy old Soviet designs—failed completely. A raging torrent of six hundred million tons of water burst forth. Not only did it instantly wipe out the nearby settlement of Daowencheng and its ninety-six hundred inhabitants, but the breach also unleashed a chain reaction. Additional dams collapsed like dominoes as a wall of water tore downstream at thirty miles per hour, gathering volume as it went. The torrent eventually totaled six billion tons of water and destroyed sixty-one dams and levees. Within a few hours of the initial dam collapse, some 85,000 people had been killed; another 145,000 would die of starvation or disease in the immediate aftermath of the disaster.

But the most astonishing thing about this horrendous episode is this: China managed to keep it secret for twenty years. One of the nation's most densely populated provinces had been utterly devastated, with a death toll approaching *a quarter of a million people*. The symbolism could hardly be starker. Dozens of flimsy old dams collapsed, allowing water to rush through unrestrained. But at the same time, China's sturdy and ancient barriers to the free flow of information held firm, and news of the disaster barely leaked out at all.

When it happened, official media carried only vague reports of serious flooding in central China. In retrospect, the most relevant item may have been a short article in the Communist party newspaper, the *People's Daily*, which simply reported that Chinese army units were performing unspecified flood control work in Henan.

In 1987, twelve years after the fact, a limited-circulation article by Chinese hydrology specialists conveyed the scope of the event more fully. But only in 1995, when the foreign nongovernmental organization Human Rights Watch/Asia released a detailed report, did the outside world learn of it. I will never forget the matter-of-fact response I got when I called China's Ministry of Water Resources to seek confirmation of that report. Why, yes, the ministry spokesman said, such an incident had in fact occurred twenty years earlier, and while he could not confirm the specific casualty counts, he did not deny them, either. It was indeed a very large and very serious event, he said, and Chinese hydrologists and engineers had learned valuable lessons from the disaster. Subsequent dam projects, the spokesman assured me, were far safer.

Such a scenario—the near-total cover-up of a massive disaster taking place just five hundred miles from Beijing—is simply unimaginable today. The reasons are partly to do with changing official policies—but only partly. Though Chinese officials continually speak of the need to improve openness, old habits are proving hard to break. For example, in a move it portrayed as an important step toward transparency and honest government, China announced in September 2005 that its National Administration of State Secrets would liberalize its reporting of disasters and declassify disaster-related death tolls. The fact that China even *has* a National Administration of State Secrets already tells you something, and no one was surprised at what happened just two months after the announcement of this small step toward Chinese glasnost.

An explosion at a chemical plant in northeastern Jilin Province had released one hundred tons of toxic benzene and other chemicals into the Songhua River, and as all that deadly poison was slowly making its way to the drinking water supply of more than three million residents of the downstream city of Harbin (and beyond that, toward Russia), government officials lied and dissembled for more than a week about what was really happening.

Cover-ups like these continue to be routine in China. They not only infuriate residents, but also leave them wondering about the accuracy of official reports on other public health threats such as air pollution, food safety, HIV/AIDS, severe acute respiratory syndrome, and avian influenza.

But the biggest changes in China's information landscape have less to do with government transparency policies and the degree to which officials do or do not follow them. Far more important is the changing reality on the ground, shaped by more than two decades of development, liberalization, and economic reform.

Across China, even in relatively remote areas, people are now linked with cell phones and Internet connections. Busy thumbs can tap out an SMS message and send it across the country—or around the world—in mere seconds. And in most locations, China's once onerous travel restrictions are also a thing of the past. So people, together with information, can come and go more freely than ever before, despite the still-common attempts by local officials to keep bad news quiet.

This discussion of how China tries—and increasingly fails—to limit the spread of bad news provides a useful backdrop to understanding the changing Chinese information environment.

Obviously, the information you'll most want to get your hands on will not be about disasters and problems in far-off corners of the country. Instead it will be news you can use about the people, places, and companies you're doing business with. Who's up and who's down in a local corruption scandal or political power struggle? Which firms are facing management shake-ups or regulatory pressure? Or it'll be market-related data affecting your own operations—consumption patterns, resource availability, growth projections, and sales and output figures in your particular sector. The list goes on and on, and such information is becoming more accessible all the time.

But as you go about the vital (and still difficult) business of gathering all that data, it is worth remembering where things stood for thousands of years in China. Because information could be either damaging to those who let it out or valuable to those who received it, it was always closely held. From one dynasty to the next, China's imperial rulers saw no need to share information publicly, and common people have long been accustomed to being kept in the dark. In 1949, the Communists who came to power brought with them not only the traditional Chinese penchant for secrecy, but also an overlay of Leninist intrigue and bureaucracy, which only served to reinforce the tendency to conceal and compartmentalize information.

I well remember a simple but illuminating example of this tendency. It was in the mid-1990s, and my family had just returned to Beijing from a few weeks of leave spent in the United States, where my young children had happily discovered the built-in children's playgrounds found at many McDonald's restaurants. At the time, McDonald's shops were sprouting up all over Beijing, too, and when my kids saw workers clearing a large space in front of one, they immediately wondered whether the workers were preparing to install a new play area.

Outgoing and inquisitive as usual, my kids asked the workers what they were doing, but the workers could only answer that they were clearing the space and digging a hole. That was what they were told to do, and sure enough, that was what they were doing. It might be for a playground, a parking lot, a flower bed, or a set of new water pipes for all they knew. They had no idea what the hole was for, or how their work would fit into any other aspect of the project.

While it hardly seems possible that a crew of American workers could do a job like that without knowing why, it struck these Chinese workers as perfectly natural. After all, they were not paid to design the project or plan it out, so why did they need to know? On the contrary: From their point of view, it seemed strange that we expected them to know anything more than they did. And even if they had, they would have found it equally odd that complete strangers—foreigners, no less— might just walk up to them cold and expect to be told about it. For me, meanwhile, it was another reminder of just how different the American and Chinese modes—and expectations—of information sharing can be.

With all this in mind, it becomes easier to comprehend how something like the 1975 Henan dam disaster could be kept quiet for so long. Or how and why, even today, Chinese officials and business counterparts may seem so reluctant to provide you with the most basic of information. It is also worth remembering that changes in the old way of doing things began only a few short decades ago, and there is still a very long way to go.

HUGE FLOOD, *LOTS* OF INFORMATION

Now that things are changing, what are the most important sources of information about what is really going on in China? They cover a wide range, all with different slants and emphases. They include local and international media, international agencies, domestic industry associations, foreign trade groups and chambers of commerce, and corporate financial reporting by individual companies.

But for basic information—the elemental building blocks of all economic and business-related data about China—the most comprehensive regular reporting by far comes from the National Bureau of Statistics (NBS). As an agency under China's State Council, the NBS manages and coordinates statistical reporting networks from provincial-, municipal-, and township-level governments, and also from individual enterprises. Much of the data you will find in other sources—other Chinese government agencies, outside analysts, or domestic and foreign media reports—will have originally come from the NBS.

Each year, the NBS publishes the *China Statistical Yearbook*, a massive doorstop of a reference book that typically runs to almost a thousand pages and reports detailed data on just about every conceivable economic, social, and geographic category. All that data takes a long time to compile, and each year's edition is only issued around September of the following year. It includes trade figures, income figures, industrial and agricultural output, investment statistics, energy and resource usage and availability, demographic data, and much, much more. In table after fine-print table, data is broken down in minute detail—by province, by city, and by sector. For many categories, information is provided with matching historical data sets going back twenty years or more.

In addition to being comprehensive, the statistical year-book is well organized and well indexed. It is also entirely bilingual, in English and Chinese. Recent editions even come with a CD-ROM full of Excel-compatible data files. The latest edition is priced at RMB 298, or about $37. The NBS maintains an English-language Web site at www.stats.gov.cn/english; and the *China Statistical Yearbook* can be ordered via e-mail to yearbook@stats.gov.cn. The book is also available at bookstores across China.

ONE FROM COLUMN A, TWO FROM COLUMN B: CHINESE COOKING ... (OF THE BOOKS!)

Regardless of what business you're in, the yearbook is a well-priced and indispensable resource. If, for example, you would like to know the province-by-province breakdown of the number of travel agencies and their related staff in China, this is the place to find it. What if you want to track the average load of Chinese railway freight cars going back to 1952? It's in there. Or maybe you're in the construction or real estate business, and you'd like to see some figures on the amount of newly built residential floor space completed in each Chinese province in each of the past twenty years. You can look it up in the yearbook. For more current data on many basic topics, you can also turn to the less comprehensive but still very useful statistical bulletins of economic and other data that the NBS releases each month. Much of that material is also available online and in English at the NBS Web site.

In addition to the general NBS yearbook, there are also many specialized yearbooks published by ministries and government departments on individual sectors, such as agriculture, power, ports, railways, IT, and more. These tend to be in Chinese only, and also tend to be much more expensive, with prices ranging as high $100 for some of them.

Once you find yourself swimming in this fine-print torrent of statistical data, the question quickly becomes: Just how reliable is it all? Unfortunately, the raw statistical data supplied by official government agencies can be spotty, inconsistent, or suspect. And sometimes it is just flat-out bogus. Since foreign economists and analysts all rely heavily on that official data, they are unavoidably handicapped. And if you are doing business in China, so are you.

As an obvious example of faulty data, consider the government's regular reporting of what is perhaps the single most important economic indicator: the gross domestic product growth rate. China puts no greater store in any other indicator. For better or worse, it is widely viewed by Chinese policy makers and business people alike as the key barometer of the nation's economic health.

Just about anyone you meet in the course of doing business in China can tell you last year's GDP growth rate, and the latest official projection for the current year's. In 2005, a top Wall Street economics guru, Stephen Roach of Morgan Stanley, gave a talk at Beijing University to an audience full of eager Chinese MBA students, and their follow-up questions zeroed in on one point alone: his projection of 6.7 percent

growth for the following year, far below China's official estimate at the time.

Roach had merely mentioned that projection as an aside
in the course of his characteristically cogent analysis of China's macroeconomic situation. He spoke convincingly of
China's need to cut fixed asset investment, reduce its reliance
on exports, bulk up its service sector, and stimulate domestic
consumption. But that lowball GDP projection of his got far
and away the most attention of anything he spoke about.

Despite this kind of obsessive concern over GDP growth
rates—which is reflected at every level of the system—the
official reporting on this most basic indicator simply fails to
add up. In most reporting periods over the past several years,
every single Chinese province has reported a growth rate
that was higher than the overall national rate. This regular
occurrence, a mathematical impossibility, has been dubbed
by some as China's "Lake Wobegon Effect," for the famous
public radio broadcaster Garrison Keillor's idyllic but ficti-
tious Minnesota town where "all of the children are above
average."

Have a look at the figures released for October 2005, for
example. They show an annualized nationwide growth rate
of 9.5 percent (see table 5.1). Now look more closely at the
growth rates reported for individual provinces. The figure
for *every single province* was higher. Most provinces showed
increases in the 12 to 14 percent range, while many were
higher still. Even the single lowest provincial figure came in at
10.4 percent, well above that 9.5 percent nationwide average.

TABLE 5.1

Economic Indicators Oct. 2005
Main Economic Indicators by Region

Region	Gross Domestic Product (Year 2004)		Value Added of Industry				Sales Ratio of Indus-trial Prod-ucts (%)
			2005. 1–9		2005. 9		
	(100 million yuan)	Growth Rate (%)	(100 million yuan)	Growth Rate (%)	(100 million yuan)	Growth Rate (%)	
Whole nation	136,875.9	9.5	50,449.9	16.3	6,275.3	16.5	98.31
Beijing	4,283.3	13.2	1,273.4	13.2	161.6	14.6	97.75
Tianjin	2,931.9	15.7	1,298.7	21.2	165.8	25.0	100.40
Hebei	8,768.8	12.5	2,373.7	23.4	300.1	25.1	98.62
Shanxi	3,042.4	14.1	1,239.0	20.0	148.9	19.5	95.37
Inner Mongolia	2,712.1	19.4	759.4	30.9	108.8	31.0	95.48
Liaoning	6,872.7	12.8	2,126.5	20.5	262.8	19.2	96.23
Jilin	2,958.2	12.2	864.7	8.0	106.6	11.9	100.89
Heilongjiang	5,303.0	11.7	1,601.8	15.0	194.0	16.5	97.61
Shanghai	7,450.3	13.6	2,959.0	12.4	355.1	15.5	99.46
Jiangsu	15,403.2	14.9	5,962.6	22.5	726.8	22.2	98.23
Zhejiang	11,243.0	14.3	3,826.3	18.1	481.9	17.6	98.22
Anhui	4,812.7	12.5	1,002.1	22.9	123.4	23.3	97.21
Fujian	6,053.1	12.1	1,664.4	18.2	199.1	19.6	99.60
Jiangxi	3,495.9	13.2	572.6	23.0	72.8	23.3	99.24
Shandong	15,490.7	15.3	6,509.8	28.4	818.5	28.7	98.47
Henan	8,815.1	13.7	2,349.8	23.4	308.0	23.6	98.69
Hubei	6,309.9	11.3	1,440.2	19.2	169.0	18.3	96.91
Hunan	5,612.3	12.0	1,106.3	21.0	138.5	20.4	100.32
Guangdong	16,039.5	14.2	6,235.1	16.8	766.2	17.7	98.60
Guangxi	3,320.1	11.8	521.1	21.0	60.8	20.0	102.10
Hainan	769.4	10.4	92.5	17.9	9.8	5.4	103.70
Chongqing	2,665.4	12.2	476.1	15.5	56.5	15.6	97.76
Sichuan	6,556.0	12.7	1,483.6	23.5	185.8	27.1	96.95
Guizhou	1,591.9	11.4	394.5	16.5	50.0	15.3	96.78
Yunnan	2,959.5	11.5	739.0	7.6	93.3	20.0	103.42
Tibet	211.5	12.2	11.2	11.4	1.5	-2.2	102.61
Shaanxi	2,883.5	12.9	798.5	18.9	105.2	20.8	93.44
Gansu	1,558.9	10.9	450.5	19.2	54.3	18.3	95.63
Qinghai	465.7	12.3	126.5	22.8	16.7	24.7	91.38
Ningxia	460.4	11.0	146.3	19.1	18.3	19.2	95.84
Xinjiang	2,200.2	11.1	657.2	18.1	88.4	9.4	97.56

NOTE: Since the GDP is calculated separately by the state and local governments, the sum of the data of different regions is not equal to the national total amount.

SOURCE: National Bureau of Statistics of China, *China Statistical Yearbook: Monthly Economic Indicators* Oct., 2005.

The anomaly is matter-of-factly acknowledged in a footnote, but nowhere is it adequately explained. Indeed, how could it be? Somehow, something in these numbers isn't right.

Blatant inaccuracies of this kind can be attributed in part to simple technical shortcomings on the part of statisticians, especially at the lower levels of small-town governments and individual enterprises. The NBS has been working hard to improve the technical standards of its data gathering and reporting. It now conducts more random checks on reported figures and gathers more of its data on its own, instead of relying on self-reporting from the lowest levels. It is also investing more in training its personnel to raise quality standards nationwide.

But beyond these technical problems of methodology, which will take years to resolve, there are also many willful distortions of data in China. In some cases, officials may twist data to show that they have achieved the growth targets or output expectations set for them by their superiors. In other cases, enterprise managers may submit lowball numbers to minimize their tax exposure, or even to conceal illicit sources of revenue.

Even data as basic as daily temperature reports have been systematically falsified in China. Chinese labor laws nominally require that workers be sent home if temperatures exceed 40 degrees Celsius (104 degrees Fahrenheit), but rather than lose a day's worth of industrial production, city officials in many industrial centers have developed a habit of reporting highs of 39 degrees to keep the factories going.

China has been cracking down on data distortion for some time, and the NBS has been making concrete efforts here as well. It punished nineteen thousand people in 2001 alone after discovering sixty thousand violations of the national statistics law. But because officials at all levels are primarily evaluated on their ability to meet their targets, and because their career prospects depend so heavily on those evaluations, the cooking of books remains rampant.

This is simply a fact of life in China, and something you need to keep in mind as you vacuum up all that increasingly available and conveniently packaged information. If it's any consolation, rest assured that your competition is dealing with the same handicap.

GOING TO WORK WITH THE DATA YOU HAVE, NOT THE DATA YOU MIGHT WANT TO HAVE

Unfortunately, outsiders have few alternatives to using China's faulty official data. Even huge multilateral organizations such as the World Bank (WB), the Asian Development Bank (ADB), the International Monetary Fund (IMF), and the United Nations Development Program (UNDP)—all of which have ample resources and talented staff economists and analysts on the ground in China—are unable to replicate the job of gathering all that information from all across this vast country. The same applies to the analysts working for foreign governments at dozens of embassies in Beijing, the journalists who write much of what you read about China, and the prognosticators and private economists who try to read the tea leaves for some of the world's largest banks and brokerage houses.

At the same time, though, none of these people can do their jobs without data. So they do the best they can working with the data they have. They are all aware of the pitfalls, and most work on the assumption that the distortions remain more or less constant from year to year. If net values cannot necessarily be trusted, these analysts usually assume that upward or downward movements in data at least reflect the real direction of any given statistical trend.

Some try to do better by using certain types of isolated data that they consider more reliable. Several years ago, Professor Thomas G. Rawski, a China specialist at the University of Pittsburgh's Economics Department, made something of a splash in the China-watching community when he examined the relationships among a number of factors, including energy usage, freight volumes, and inventory accumulations, to triangulate a more plausible figure for China's GDP. He concluded that China's economic growth rate for 2001 was probably closer to 4 percent than the 7.3 percent figure reported by the government.

Other economists prefer to use isolated data that can be cross-checked against other sources, such as external trade figures, to make their own estimates about what's really going on in the Chinese economy.

Like these macro analysts, you too will need to keep your skeptical antennae primed for anomalies and distortions in the information you do manage to get hold of. And since you presumably have the added advantage of understanding your own sector, you should be well equipped to spot the little things that just don't make sense.

While trying to analyze China's livestock and meat sector, for example, agricultural specialists at the Organization for Economic Cooperation and Development (OECD) noticed that the reported supply of animal feed in China did not match the demand that was implied elsewhere in the data. By picking apart the published statistics and recalculating on the basis of the numbers that could be more readily confirmed—and were therefore more likely to be accurate—these data sleuths concluded that the true figure for urban per capita meat consumption in China was probably two to three times higher than had been reported. For anyone working in the animal feed, livestock, or meat distribution industry, such an insight would be valuable indeed.

EVERYBODY'S SURFING . . . SURFING PRC!

China's leading general Web portals are also putting up more and more of their content in English, and the country's two main sites, Sohu.com and Sina.com, will probably end up on your Internet bookmark list before long. Their English-language pages can be found at http://english.sohu.com and http://english.sina.com/index.html. While much of their front-page news content overlaps with that of the *China Daily*, their search engines lead to many English-language Chinese sources that would be otherwise hard to find. These portals, of course, labor under the same restrictions as all other Chinese media, which means there are limits to what your searches will turn up. But on the plus side, links that do appear through these sites are not banned by government censors and will therefore allow you to click through. The same applies to www.baidu.com, China's leading homegrown search engine.

It is a common and frustrating experience in China to find that many links found through Google or other mainstream Western search engines are blocked by government censors. In some of these cases, where the sites carry content about sensitive political issues such as Taiwan, Tibet, or Chinese political dissidents, the reasons are obvious and unsurprising, even if they are disagreeable to Western sensibilities.

In other cases, seemingly innocuous content is blocked by China's vast data filtering system—the so-called Great Firewall of China. Interestingly, there are nominally procedures in place by which users may apply to have access be restored to sites that have been mistakenly classified as "objectionable" or "inappropriate" by China's mysterious Internet gatekeepers. But since these gatekeepers work in secret, the requests must go through a commercial Internet service provider, and it is not clear that many of them ever succeed.

Like China's more savvy Web users, foreign residents in China often find their way around the government 'Net nanny by using various proxy servers. The most effective require a subscription fee and can sometimes slow down data transfers or interfere with other computer applications such as chat programs. And even without a proxy, you will find that all that Chinese data packet inspection slows your surfing considerably.

But despite all this maddening filtering, Web surfing in China remains a vital tool. Chinese government departments got off to a slow start in establishing their Web presence, with many ministries and agencies making halfhearted stop-and-go efforts that produced shabby Web sites. Never very useful to begin with, some of these are still lingering around the Web like so much outdated cyberspace junk. More recently, though, government Web sites are coming up to speed. In 2005, the central government launched its official English-language Web gateway at http://english.gov.cn. Providing up-to-date links to business information, statistics, and updates on China's rapidly changing laws, the site is another excellent resource.

The city of Beijing has also gotten into the act with its own gateway, www.ebeijing.gov.cn, which provides some vital nuts-and-bolts information about living as a foreign resident in the Chinese capital.

FOREIGN WEB RESOURCES

Apart from mainstream foreign media sites, there is a wealth of information about China available online from international agencies. Among the best are the China pages of the World Bank (http://web.worldbank.org) and the Asian Development Bank (www.adb.org). Both provide massive amounts of valuable information about China's macroeconomic situation and in-depth resources on specific sectors. Similar offerings can be found at sites belonging to the United Nations (www.unchina.org), International Monetary Fund (www .imf.org), and Organization for Economic Cooperation and Development (www.oecd.org).

HOT OFF THE PRESSES

Another potentially important source of information about China is the domestic media. This was not always the case, and it may well come as a surprise to anyone with an outdated view of the Chinese media industry.

When I first got to China in the late 1980s, the publishing scene was indeed dreary and monochromatic. I was then working at a British news bureau that received dozens of local papers every day, and the content was barely distinguishable from one paper to the next. This was predictable, since much of that content came from the same state-run Xinhua News Agency, and most of the editorial decision making came trickling down from the same central government propaganda office.

Because the papers were heavily subsidized, and also because their subscribers were usually government offices or state-run enterprises that had no choice in the matter, publishers cared little about producing interesting content or eye-catching covers. These papers were of course a vital tool for keeping up with the official line, but they seldom provided much else in the way of useful information.

But like just about everything else in China, the media business has undergone huge changes in the last ten years. The market is now flooded with new titles, all engaged in cut-throat competition for eyeballs and for advertising dollars. Look out your taxicab window from any street corner in any Chinese city, and you are sure to spot a newsstand crowded with papers and magazines featuring flashy graphics, sensational headlines, and plenty of sex appeal.

Nationwide, there are now more than eight thousand magazines, two thousand newspapers, and three hundred television stations competing for over $35 billion in annual advertising spending. With tens of millions of Chinese taking their chances in the domestic stock markets and millions more in business for themselves, business news ranks right up there with fashion, lifestyle, and sports as a top seller.

To meet this demand, Chinese reporters are digging into stories in ways that were once unimaginable. Of course, all Chinese media remain under direct government control, and all must still abide by some fairly burdensome restrictions as to what they may or may not publish—especially about the people and policies at the highest levels of government. As a result, most Chinese reporters live with the frustration of knowing that their juiciest stories will never see the light of day.

Unofficial interference can be even uglier. In its crudest form, Chinese reporters are routinely subjected to threats, and sometimes actual violence, when their reporting leads them to influential people who have something to hide.

And sometimes the interference is more subtle. I know of a television news reporter at a leading Chinese network whose career hit a dead end after he followed up a lead on a banking corruption scandal. Recognizing the need to rein in rampant corruption and the potential usefulness of news media in exposing it, the Chinese government has grown somewhat more tolerant of this kind of reporting. So it was not entirely unreasonable to think he might well uncover a blockbuster story that he could actually air on his news program.

But after just a bit of digging, he realized it involved very senior figures in the Beijing municipal security apparatus. Airing a story would be out of the question. And since digging any further would be at best a waste of time, and would at worst lead to serious trouble, he prudently decided to leave the story alone.

For any reporter, dropping a huge scoop would be frustrating enough, but unfortunately for this reporter, those implicated in the scandal had gotten wind of his preliminary efforts and were not content to take his word that he planned to leave it alone. Instead, they sought to guarantee his silence by co-opting him with bribes. The offers escalated quickly, from cash, to a small downtown apartment, and eventually to a house in the suburbs.

In response to his principled refusal to accept, these nervous officials mounted a yearlong campaign of threats, bullying, and harassment. The news unit has seen its funding and airtime dry up. The reporter's colleagues and fiancée have likewise been harassed and intimidated. Seeing no sign that he has persuaded his adversaries to let up, he has instead had to give serious thought to leaving China altogether.

Yet even in this environment, reporters do manage to produce some fairly edgy work. One of the favorite tactics of muckraking Chinese journalists is to keep their noses out of touchy issues close to their home turf. The sort of people who intimidated my friend tend to have considerable localized clout, but only limited reach into other places. A reporter from another province stands a much better chance of following through on an investigation and getting a story out.

So despite the limitations on how and where they can work freely, Chinese media outlets are putting out some important and revealing information that can be very useful to you as you seek to keep up with developments in the places or the sectors you're involved with. If, for example, an official gets taken down in a corruption scandal in a city where you're doing business, that is something you need to know—and more and more frequently, news like that gets broken first in the local Chinese press.

Only a tiny fraction of this output is ever published in English, so if you do not read Chinese yourself, you need to find another way to keep up with it all. One way is to task a member of your local staff with making a regular scan of the local press for items of interest to your business. Since most major Chinese publications now have a Web presence, it's easier than ever to keep up with what is being written about particular companies, whether they are your suppliers, competitors, or even partners.

But if you do go this route, it is vital that you provide clear and specific guidance as to what you think is important. Such local staffers all too often assume that the most important stories are the big banner headlines simultaneously carried by major official media outlets. In a way, of course, these stories are important, since they represent the government point of view. But those items are also easily accessible, even in China's official English-language publications, so in order to really add value for you, staffers need to develop an eye for picking out the unusual and meaty tidbits that are relevant to your business.

Another option is to outsource the job to a professional media monitoring service. Public relations firms, both major international ones and their local competitors, offer such services to their clients in China. There are also companies that perform customized monitoring of Chinese media. Among them are SinoFile.net (www.sinofile.net), Miaojian Information Ltd. (www.miaojian.com), and EIN News (www.einnews .com/china).

Regardless of whether you outsource the bulk of your media monitoring work or handle it in-house, you should also make it a point to keep yourself up to speed with China's increasingly abundant English-language media sources. The national English-language *China Daily* newspaper is one place to start.

Though it is often disparaged as a government mouthpiece (which it is), it is nevertheless a useful resource. The *China Daily* is also widely ridiculed by some jaded foreign readers for its relentlessly upbeat boosterism of government policies. While there is truth in this criticism, the paper has also ventured into cautious coverage of the darker side of the China story. Overall, it provides a solid roundup of the government line on the most important issues, and despite the fact that it is aimed at a foreign audience and therefore has a slightly different slant, it does provide a representative taste of what mainstream Chinese media are like. The paper itself is widely distributed throughout China, often for free. Subscriptions for same-day delivery within China are very cheap, and just about all of its content, including archived material, is available free online at www.chinadaily.net.

Other useful English-language domestic outlets include the state-run Xinhua News Agency (www.xinhuanet.com/english), which is searchable and updated constantly, and the *Beijing Review* (www.bjreview.com), which carries lengthier features and analyses (but again, with a distinctly official flavor and pro-government stamp).

Some of the more recent arrivals on the Chinese media scene are far more interesting, and leading that pack is *Caijing Magazine*. With its title meaning "finance and economics," *Caijing* was founded in 1998 as a monthly and quickly became a must-read in Chinese business and policy circles and beyond. Though it is still subject to state supervision, the magazine remains remarkably independent by Chinese standards. Edited by an impressive go-getter of a woman named Hu Shuli, *Caijing* is now published every two weeks and runs some of China's edgiest reporting on business affairs, politics, and social issues. A portion of its content is available in English at http://caijing.hexun.com/english/home.aspx and is well worth reading, not only for its own sake, but also because it drives a lot of the watercooler conversation at companies and government offices throughout China. *Caijing* is widely and faithfully read by Chinese decision makers and business people, and reading it yourself is a good way to know a little something extra about what goes into the thinking of the people you're dealing with.

While you will certainly want to make use of China's increasingly rich media environment, you must also be aware of the shortcomings. Chinese journalists unfortunately have a fair bit in common with Chinese statisticians, and their craft is not always practiced to the highest technical or ethical standards. Relatively new to the business of digging for real news, many Chinese journalists are often content to rely on government or corporate handouts, relaying them to readers with little value added.

Worse still, many are happy to run positive stories for any company that is willing to pay them. An American executive once told me what happened at the follow-up interview requested by a Chinese journalist who attended her company's news conference several years ago. Rather than ask more questions, he instead made a simple offer: For 5,000 RMB, he would write a positive story about the company; for 10,000 he would let her write it herself, then see to it that it ran prominently in his newspaper. So yet again, a standard piece of conventional wisdom—"You can't believe everything you read"—also applies in China. Only more so.

CORPORATE INFORMATION

If you can't always believe what you read in the Chinese press, what about the information that Chinese companies release directly? Fortunately, this is one area where the nation is making rapid progress, especially among its listed companies. The Chinese government is making a huge push toward improving the standards of corporate governance, and a big part of that effort centers on enforcing the accuracy of corporate financial reporting. Leading the way are the many Chinese firms who have listed on US and other overseas markets. Subject to these more stringent requirements, the firms are helping set a higher overall standard nationwide.

Here, too, it is useful to compare the current situation with the not-too-distant past. China's two domestic stock exchanges, in Shenzhen and Shanghai, were launched in 1990 and 1991, and in the first few years the standards of financial reporting were simply atrocious. During that period, I saw a tiny notice placed in a local newspaper in which a company announced that the financial statement it had released several days before contained an error. Instead of *earning* several million yuan in the previous quarter, as it had stated, the firm had actually *lost* several million yuan. The firm cordially apologized to investors for the unfortunate error, and for any inconvenience it might have caused.

The consequences for such shenanigans have since grown more severe. A landmark case occurred in late 2002, when Shanghai-listed retailer Zhengzhou Baiwen falsified its financials and overstated profits to pump up its stock price. Three executives were convicted in criminal court, and the firm also faced civil suits filed by aggrieved investors. Since then, auditing standards have been made more stringent still. While Chinese firms do not yet have to deal with anything as onerous as the Sarbanes-Oxley Act, they are responding to the pressure with more accurate reporting.

SEEING IS BELIEVING

In China, like anywhere else, the best way to find out what's going on is to see for yourself. One of the most astute China analysts around is Jing Ulrich, head of China markets for JPMorgan Securities. As someone who makes her living evaluating Chinese equities, she long ago realized that media reports, company filings, and even secondhand anecdotes about Chinese firms give only an incomplete picture. "What I've learned," Ulrich told me, "is that you need to travel. You need to talk to people directly, and most of all you need to get in there and kick the tires for yourself."

As a Beijing native, Ulrich can do a lot of that legwork herself. Non-Chinese-speakers, though, need help from local colleagues. But unfortunately, sending locals in search of information in China sometimes entails serious pitfalls. China maintains wide-ranging and sometimes quite arbitrary rules on what exactly constitutes a state secret, and over the years many Chinese employees of Western firms have learned—the hard way—that poking around for sensitive business-related information could land them on the wrong side of the law.

There were numerous such cases in the mid-1990s. One involved Xiu Yichun, a Chinese executive working for the Royal Dutch Shell oil company. When she tried to learn details of the pending government approval process on a large refinery project her company was jointly developing with the China National Offshore Oil Corporation, she landed in Chinese legal limbo, detained but not charged. She was released, but only after thirteen months.

At around the same time, a local researcher for the Swiss securities firm SBC Warburg found herself in a similar plight after finding out a little bit too much about Chinese central bank plans for a currency devaluation. In a similar case,

Chinese researcher Xi Yang was working for an overseas newspaper and was sentenced to twelve years in jail for obtaining and divulging restricted information about Chinese gold production figures and interest rate policies.

More recently, ethnic Chinese social scientists, including many with foreign passports, have landed in jail because their research crossed the murky lines China uses to define its "secrets." There have been fewer such cases in recent years, but the threat remains very real. Chinese materials are often marked SECRET or INTERNAL CIRCULATION ONLY even though they are widely available. Even certain newspapers, such as the *Cankao Xiaoxi*, "reference news," are classified this way, despite the fact that they are openly sold at sidewalk kiosks for mere pennies.

But foreign companies can take steps to protect their local employees from these dangers, according to longtime American China hand John Kamm, who speaks from vast personal experience.

Kamm made his first trip to China in 1976 and went on to develop a career as a very successful (and very well-paid) executive. But starting in 1990, he began putting his China expertise to work on human rights cases, lobbying for the release of political prisoners. He eventually shifted out of business altogether and founded the San Francisco–based Dui Hua (dialogue) Foundation, working full time to research the cases of political prisoners and advocate on their behalf. He has had a remarkable string of successful interventions, helping secure the release of numerous prisoners while at the same time maintaining good relations with his many high-ranking Chinese contacts.

According to Kamm, foreign firms need to recognize the special risks faced by their ethnic Chinese executives and tread carefully in terms of what they ask them to do. They also need to be prepared with a rapid response plan in case the worst does happen.

In Chinese criminal law, the status of detainees changes quickly in the first few days after arrest, and the deeper a case goes into the process, the harder it is to slow the legal machinery that almost always produces convictions. In the time it might take a company to figure out which lawyer to call in and which government officials to go to for help, a case can move irretrievably down the line. Companies therefore need to know ahead of time exactly what to do, and then move quickly to get it done.

KEY POINTS TO REMEMBER
FROM CHAPTER 5

1. Culturally and politically, the default tendency in China is toward secrecy rather than openness and information sharing. Things are improving all the time, but getting access to relevant and accurate information about the Chinese business environment will be one of your key challenges.

2. For the most elemental economic and business-related data about China, the National Bureau of Statistics is a prime source. Each year, it publishes the *China Statistical Yearbook,* a bilingual compilation

of detailed data on just about every conceivable economic, social, and geographic category. The NBS also maintains a bilingual Web site and publishes other useful resources, including monthly statistical updates.

3. Unfortunately, the quality of raw statistical data supplied by official government agencies in China can be spotty, ranging from vaguely inconsistent to downright bogus. Most analysts work on the assumption that the distortions tend to remain constant from year to year, and that even if reported net values cannot be trusted, upward or downward movements in data at least reflect the real direction of any given statistical trend.

4. The Internet in China is tightly censored. Content is controlled on domestic Web sites, and "the Great Firewall of China" blocks access to many foreign Web sites. Nevertheless, the Internet remains a valuable resource. Many Chinese government agencies maintain useful sites, and despite the frustrations of the blockages, a lot of foreign sites remain accessible.

5. Strict limits on press freedom notwithstanding, Chinese media sometimes carry important and revealing information that can help you keep up with developments in the places and sectors you're involved with. If, say, a corruption scandal shakes things up in a city where you're doing business, you need to know about it. These days, such news sometimes breaks first in the local Chinese press.

6. If you do not read Chinese yourself, you will need to find another way to keep up with local media. You can either task a member of your local staff with making a regular scan of the local press for items of interest to your business, or outsource the job to one of the media monitoring companies working in China.

7. Standards of corporate and financial reporting are improving but remain lax by Western standards. The best way to find out about a company is to check it out in person and "kick the tires" yourself.

8. Despite moves toward openness, stern secrecy laws remain in place in China. Foreign firms can and have run afoul of these laws, with severe consequences. Local employees are especially vulnerable to legal problems.

USEFUL CHINA-RELATED WEB SITES

Chinese Government Web Sites

Central Government of China: http://english.gov.cn
China's Ministry of Commerce: http://english.mofcom.gov.cn
City of Beijing: www.ebeijing.gov.cn
City of Shanghai: www.shanghai.gov.cn
National Bureau of Statistics: www.stats.gov.cn/english

Chinese Web Portals and Leading Media Sites

Baidu: www.baidu.com
Beijing Review: www.bjreview.com

Caijing Magazine: http://caijing.hexun.com/english/home.aspx
China Daily: www.chinadaily.com.cn
Sina: http://english.sina.com/index.html
Sohu: http://english.sohu.com
Xinhua News Agency: www.xinhua.net/english

China-Related Web Sites of US Organizations

American Chamber of Commerce in China: www.amcham-china
.org.cn
United States embassy, Beijing: http://beijing.usembassy-china
.org.cn
US–China Business Council: www.uschina.org

China-Related Web Sites of International Agencies

Asian Development Bank: www.adb.org
International Monetary Fund: www.imf.org
Organization for Economic Cooperation and Development:
www.oecd.org
United Nations: www.unchina.org
World Bank: http://web.worldbank.org

6

The China Price

In an influential article published in December 2004, *Business Week* magazine identified what it called "the three scariest words in U.S. industry." Those three simple words? *The China Price.*

"In general," *Business Week* explained, the China Price "means 30% to 50% less than what you can possibly make something for in the U.S. In the worst cases, it means below your cost of materials."

Scary stuff indeed. In his 2004 book *The Chinese Century,* Oded Shenkar offered an ominous warning, saying that "the dislocations brought about by China's advance are not cyclical and temporary but represent a fundamental restructuring of the global business system." He also offered some very stark advice: "For firms that operate in labor-intensive industries, the writing is on the wall. For many developed-country firms, especially those lacking the pricing power of brand or specialized capabilities, the best option is simply to exit the market.

"This is a harsh remedy with ominous consequences for employees and communities, but one that may be preferable to slow bleeding because it avails capital and human resources to be redeployed rather than exhausted," continued Shenkar, who is chair of global business management at the Ohio State University's Fisher College of Business.

Some thirteen years before Shenkar wrote those words, I was taken on an impromptu walking tour of the China Price phenomenon by my own father-in-law, Morris Lipson, who even then was already grappling with it. He had spent years building and running a clothing business that was headquartered in Manhattan and manufactured inexpensive women's clothing—robes, housedresses, and dusters—at one factory in Virginia and another in North Carolina. In January 1992, the day after the birth of our first son, my wife asked me to run out and bring back a sweater to her hospital room, and Morris came along with me to a Kmart near the hospital in South Florida.

I was eager to grab a sweater quickly and get right back to the hospital, but Morris kept stopping every few steps, inspecting one garment after another. He looked at the prices and muttered the same thing every time: "How do they do it? How can I compete with them at these prices?" All the least expensive items he'd been looking at on those racks were made in China, and he quickly calculated that he could not bring raw fabric into his factory door at those prices, much less get a product out—or earn a profit on it. A few short years later, both his factories were shuttered.

Even then, of course, there was nothing new in the challenge posed by low-cost foreign producers. It has been a major factor in the loss of millions of American manufacturing jobs over recent decades. And it hasn't just been China. Like other Americans in his industry, Morris was also competing with cheap garment producers in Latin America, Egypt, Bangladesh, and elsewhere. In other industries, American manufacturers were struggling to compete with the influx of cheap footwear from Vietnam, cheap consumer electronics from Malaysia, and thousands of other cheap products—ranging from toys to furniture—from dozens of other developing countries.

But yet again, China presents a special case. Unlike most other developing economies, China's export potential is underpinned by a vast and rapidly growing home market. The combination affords China unparalleled opportunities to leverage economies of scale, and is one of many factors that go into the making of the China Price. Through size alone, China has the potential to dominate in many sectors.

The same dynamic explains why fear and consternation were not the only Western responses to the China Price phenomenon. The combination of low-cost production opportunities and potential access to a huge market also inspired a lot of enthusiasm—and a veritable stampede of Western companies into China's manufacturing heartland in search of cost efficiencies.

For all the fear the China Price strikes in the hearts of Western manufacturers, it is worth noting that it has also caused some hand-wringing on the Chinese side. The pressure, after all, cuts both ways, and the relentless drive of Western retailers and manufacturers for lower prices has unleashed brutal competition within China among potential suppliers. Indeed, as JPMorgan's Jing Ulrich put it, "China is still a price taker, not a price setter, because no one in China can afford to lose Wal-Mart as a customer."

STITCHING TOGETHER AN INDUSTRY LEADER

The textile and apparel sector is probably the best illustration of how China has realized its potential for industry dominance. China had already been a powerful player in the garment trade for many years, but its global competitors felt particular dread as January 1, 2005, approached. Under the rules governing China's accession to the WTO, that date would mark the end of all quota restrictions on Chinese garment exports. As it approached, producers in other developing countries sounded grim alarms about the damage an unrestrained China might do, not just to their fabric industries, but also to the fabric of their societies.

In Bangladesh, industry leaders predicted the looming Chinese threat to the jobs of that country's ten million textile workers might lead to "social anarchy." Even the WTO's own director general, Supachai Panitchpakdi, acknowledged that the economies of many developing countries might become "highly vulnerable" upon the lifting of those quotas.

During the run-up to the final lifting of quotas, Chinese officials went out of their way in public to allay fears over what they called "sensational" predictions of doom and gloom. The end of quotas, they argued, would benefit other countries, too. Any growth of China's textile industry would mean greater imports of advanced equipment, cotton, and chemical fiber products from abroad. Furthermore, because an estimated 40 percent of China's apparel exports come from international joint ventures, foreign partners would be sharing in all that wealth. "China is a major player but will not sweep the world," one Chinese textile industry official promised before the quotas were lifted.

Privately, though, many people in the Chinese textile industry were quick to tell me they thought China would indeed be hard to stop. Upon joining the WTO, the nation had agreed to lower tariffs and allow greater foreign access across virtually all sectors of its market. Many Chinese industries would feel a lot of pain as a result—among them the banking and agricultural sectors, which in particular were seen as poorly positioned to stand up to foreign competition.

But the textile sector would be different. This was one area where China simply enjoyed too many advantages. It could indeed be expected to dominate, and the world would just have to accept that fact of life as a part of the broader WTO deal.

Before looking at exactly what those advantages are and which ones foreign companies can and cannot leverage, let's see how things really panned out after those quotas were lifted at the start of 2005. The details depend a fair bit on exactly which products—and whose data—you choose to look at. Nevertheless, the trend could not be clearer.

At the end of the first quarter of 2005, the US Department of Commerce reported that American imports of Chinese textile and apparel products had risen more than 63 percent from the same period of the previous year. Around the same time, the Chinese government released statistics showing that during the first two months of 2005, the value of its global textile exports rose to almost $14 billion, a 31 percent increase over the previous year.

In its *Asian Development Outlook 2006* report, the ADB said fears that the rest of Asia's clothing industry would collapse seemed "exaggerated." But look more closely at what ADB reported: Chinese shipments to the United States and Europe had risen sharply in early 2005, and eased back only when import surge protection safeguard mechanisms were activated later in the year.

Even with the safeguard quotas, Chinese clothing claimed a 30 percent share in European markets and a 25 percent share in US markets in 2005. Meanwhile, the combined US market share of Hong Kong, Taiwan, and South Korea fell from 9.7 percent in 2004 to 6.1 percent in 2005, in terms of volume. In value terms, their share dropped from 11.1 to 8.4 percent during the same period.

But under current rules, those safeguard quotas can be used only through 2008, after which China's clothing industry will be subject to no restraints at all. A 2006 study by the National Council of Textile Organizations, a Washington-based industry group, found that China was able to win a 70 percent market share in markets where it faced no quantitative restrictions. Far from a neutral observer, NCTO works to advance the interests of the US textile sector, and it has called for changes in the WTO rules that would extend the use of protective safeguard mechanisms past 2008.

Focusing on fifty-three product categories that were removed from quotas in 2005 and were not subject to additional safeguard quotas, NCTO found that China's share of the US import market rose from 15 to 38 percent in that single year. Examining another group of fifty-three products that had seen quotas lifted at the start of 2002, NCTO reported even more dramatic findings. China's market share of US imports for these products surged from 21 percent in 2001 to more than 66 percent by 2005. During that time, producers from Mexico, Thailand, Bangladesh, the Philippines, and the Caribbean all saw their exports to the United States decline. Without an extension of safeguard protections, the NCTO report warned, China could be expected to take a 70 percent share across the board and continue "its march toward market monopolization."

It is easy to assume that China's advantage in the textile sector is solely a result of its cheap labor. In fact, it is a common misperception that labor costs alone are enough to explain the overall China Price phenomenon. Clearly, the ability of Chinese factories to hire full-time production workers for $100 per month or less plays a vital role. But since China's textile industry is taking jobs from countries like Bangladesh as well as from the United States, that is obviously not the only factor. In reality, the cost of labor is only one part of a complicated picture, and a smaller part than you probably imagine.

In 2005, analysts at CLSA reported the results of their survey of Chinese small and medium enterprises, which employ an estimated three-quarters of the nation's manufacturing workers. The survey found that for 60 percent of these enterprises, *labor accounted for one-tenth or less of their production costs.* And for only 10 percent of these enterprises did labor make up 20 percent or more of total output costs.

Clearly, then, the answer to my father-in-law's repeated question—"How do they do it?"—is not cheap labor alone. China's successful march to the top of the world garment industry has been built on much else besides. For one thing, Chinese firms have invested huge sums in the past twenty years in modernizing their operations. This marks a big change from earlier times, when the demands of Chinese consumers were uniformly low and Chinese clothing producers viewed their output as something akin to a bulk commodity.

Today some Chinese firms can still operate on that model to meet the demand of the country's own hundreds of millions of low-end consumers. At the same time, though, there are thousands of Chinese garment firms using imported state-of-the-art manufacturing equipment and the latest high-tech tools to raise their productivity and improve their design processes. There are now at least fifty Chinese universities offering textile and design degree programs, and they are turning out graduates who are better equipped to tackle the design, marketing, and product development areas of the business that so many Chinese firms in the past tended to neglect.

China's performance in foreign markets has been helped by the growing sense of fashion consciousness and rising standards of living in the nation's more prosperous areas. Shanghai emerged in the 1990s as China's own fashion capital, and it now has its sights set firmly on taking a place within the next ten years right alongside Milan, Paris, New York, and Tokyo as a worldwide fashion center. The more it learns about meeting the needs of its more sophisticated customers at home, the better positioned the Chinese garment industry is to satisfy higher-end demand in its export markets abroad.

But instead of simply vacating the low-end of the market as it moves up the value chain, China's textile industry has expanded into the higher end, all the while keeping its firm foothold along the rest of the spectrum. This marks an important difference from the path to success taken by Asia's so-called Tiger economies (Hong Kong, Singapore, South Korea, and Taiwan), which tended to abandon the lower-end segments to other low-cost producers as they moved up the chain. By broadening its footprint rather than just migrating upward, China gains huge advantages of scale.

So China has gone far beyond a simple leveraging of its cheap labor. Instead, it has built a globally dominant industry on a variety of pillars, including sound strategy and prudent investment in the sector over a long period of time.

It has followed a similar model in its production of television sets. While its domestic producers continue to thoroughly dominate the local market for standard color TV sets, China has also been expanding upward into the flat-plasma-screen market. That segment, mainly featuring products with larger screens and higher profit margins, is currently dominated by South Korean and Taiwanese producers. Many of those have already moved their manufacturing operations to China, and Chinese producers have been quick to jump into the same space with their own versions of those products. They have yet to overtake the market leaders, but they are already making rapid inroads into a segment that appears to have a bright future. According to Analysys Inc., a Chinese technology consultancy, the flat-screen TV market grew 116 percent over 2005 and is expected to grow at an average annual rate of 56 percent in the following four years.

The stars do not line up so neatly for Chinese producers in all sectors, and in some areas they face serious deficiencies. That, of course, means there are plenty of opportunities for foreign businesses to press their own advantages while accessing what they can of China's.

MANAGEMENT

Management expertise remains one area where Western firms tend to have an advantage over Chinese competitors. One good place to begin leveraging it is in the management of that much-discussed local resource: cheap unskilled labor.

Historically, Chinese manufacturing firms have never dwelled much, either in theory or in practice, on the subtleties of human resource management. Unskilled labor has largely been viewed as a commodity. It has to be paid for, and of course in China that price tag has often included extensive social welfare obligations, but it has not typically been seen as something to be cultivated, developed, or invested in. The lack of any independent labor rights movement in China has contributed to this situation. As a result, workers have been seen as nondifferentiated and easily replaceable parts of the input stream—not much different from the energy needed to run a plant or the iron ore needed to produce steel.

As any Western management theorist can tell you, however, happy employees tend to work better, and a failure to take employee satisfaction into account is sure to cut into productivity. Many Chinese enterprises tolerate low levels of dedication and poor performance from their workers. They also suffer from low retention rates and high retraining costs, and many of them, especially the old-line state-owned enterprises, tend to view these factors as part of the built-in cost of the labor resource.

It is easy enough to see how they come to this conclusion. The rural workers who flock to towns and cities in search of work tend only to stay there for limited periods. The wage differential between the towns and their rural home regions is enough to attract them, but not enough to keep them. Most come to work for a couple of years, just long enough to accumulate the cash they need to start up small businesses of their own back home.

But that may not be long enough for their employers to get optimum value out of them. The jobs being filled by so-called unskilled laborers actually cover a wide range, and the training and ramp-up times vary accordingly. It may not take long to bring workers up to efficient productivity levels if they are stitching garments or gluing sneakers together. But in other industries, things can be different. According to executives at one international cell phone handset manufacturer, it can take as long as a year to train a Chinese worker on the company's latest production equipment. In a case like that, it could be well worthwhile to try to keep that worker from leaving so soon.

Chinese firms often lack the imagination and the management tools they would need to get more value out their workers. Some of the better ones are starting to catch up on this front, but nationwide productivity increases—impressive as they are—are not yet outpacing wage increases. Between 1992 and 2006, labor productivity among urban workers has increased by a factor of five—not bad at all. But during the same period, the average urban wage in China has risen nearly *ninefold*, from about $250 per year to around $2,200.

Most Chinese enterprises have achieved their productivity improvements through increased mechanization, and they have yet to tap the productivity potential of improved management. Until they do, it leaves open an advantage for foreign firms, which tend to have a broader view of a workforce's potential value and to be more experienced in motivating employees in both financial and nonfinancial ways. This can generate significant benefits in terms of worker performance, enterprise efficiency, and product quality.

Then again, how important is it to maximize the value of this resource? After all, we have just seen that labor only represents a small proportion of production costs for most manufacturers. So is it not likely that the older Chinese approach actually makes more sense? The answer is that even if it does, it won't for much longer.

The current state of affairs, in which the labor pool seems inexhaustible and labor represents only a small proportion of costs, is already showing signs of shifting. China is of course far from running out of workers. There are tens of millions more people living in the Chinese countryside than are needed to work at agricultural jobs, and there is no reason to expect them to stop coming to towns and cities in search of more lucrative manufacturing jobs.

But in manufacturing bases such as the Pearl River and Yangtze River deltas, China is beginning to run out of a certain *type* of worker: namely, young single females who are responsible for no dependent family members, are easier to manage, and can be employed at the lowest rates of pay. As this cohort begins to get stretched thinner, factories are having to employ more men and more older people. These workers need to earn enough to support families, and they are driving labor prices up. Already, Chinese workers cost one-third more than their counterparts in neighboring Vietnam.

In spring 2005, the city of Shenzhen implemented a 23 percent increase in the monthly minimum wage for its factory workers. One of China's earliest special economic zones, Shenzhen lies in Guangdong Province, just across the border from Hong Kong, and has become one of China's leading manufacturing hubs. Having transformed itself from a nondescript fishing village of about twenty thousand people in the early 1980s to the huge and modern city of eleven million that it is today, Shenzhen has all along been a trendsetter in Chinese economic reform policies. But in this instance, it is playing catch-up with other regions.

In a situation that once seemed unimaginable for any region in China, Shenzhen is having trouble finding workers to staff its factories. The 2005 wage increase followed one ordered the previous year, and upon taking effect it upped the minimum monthly wage for Shenzhen workers from 690 yuan ($86) to around 850 yuan ($106). Even at that level, though, the Shenzhen minimum will not match that paid in and around Shanghai. And it so happens that the Shanghai area, and the Yangtze River region that sweeps westward from there, is where a lot of Guangdong's missing workers have gone. In Shenzhen alone, city officials reported a shortage of one hundred thousand workers. Estimates for the worker deficit in all of Guangdong run as high as one million.

For foreign companies, this means several things. Some are now compelled to follow in the footsteps of the many Chinese companies that have begun to move westward and inland in search of better labor pools, to areas like Sichuan and Guangxi Provinces. It also means that as the cost of labor rises across China's manufacturing base, the superior ability of foreign companies to manage and cultivate workers will become an increasingly important advantage.

There are other aspects of Chinese management styles that also put a drag on the performance of the country's companies. In a survey of the cultural practices of Chinese middle managers, Nandani Lynton and Mansour Javidan identified numerous tendencies that threaten to hold their companies back. The scholars, both of Thunderbird's Garvin School of International Management, argued that a failure to overcome these tendencies could leave China stuck in a role where its companies mainly act as subcontractors for the world's global corporations.

The traditional model of Chinese corporate leadership, for example, tends to be autocratic, and while Chinese executives are increasingly aware of the need to push decision making and responsibility farther down the line, they continue to struggle against what Lynton and Javidan called China's "long history of benevolent paternalism." All this works to stifle creativity, innovation, knowledge sharing, and entrepreneurship.

Chinese business leaders also impede cross-unit coordination and collaboration because of the traditional emphasis on "in-group" cultures. Escaping the negative impact of this tendency, Lynton and Javidan argued, will require a shift away from the focus on personal trust and toward more formal models of trust, accountability, and performance evaluation. The pair also found Chinese managers to have a negative view of "worldliness" and concluded that national pride and a determination to remain faithful to Chinese business and cultural traditions could hamper the ability of Chinese firms to optimize their interactions with the outside world.

Western companies no doubt suffer a great deal because of their deficient understanding of Chinese conditions and practices. But in the areas identified by Lynton and Javidan, they generally tend to perform far better, and as a result they can enjoy significant advantages over Chinese competitors in their flexibility, nimbleness, and efficiency.

It is, however, an advantage that they will need to tap soon, because the quality of Chinese management talent is improving rapidly. Ever since the 1980s, China has been sending its best and brightest overseas for college and graduate education. For much of that time, the vast majority chose not to come back. Of the 580,000 Chinese students and scholars who went abroad between 1978 and 2002, only 160,000 returned to China. Wherever they had gone to study—whether Canada, the United States, Europe, or Australia—these students could usually find better opportunities by staying put after finishing their studies. No one in China could offer anything approaching the compensation, working conditions, or job satisfaction that they could readily find abroad. The brain-drain issue was for many years a serious concern among top Chinese leaders, some of whom openly wondered whether it suited the nation's interests to continue supporting this outflow of talent.

By the mid-1990s, however, the tide began to turn. Between the heavy presence of foreign multinational corporations in China, and the emergence of an entirely new class of high-performance Chinese companies, many of these people were finally being tempted to return home and pursue opportunities in China.

More recently still, young Chinese graduates are deciding against going abroad for continued study, opting instead to take advantage of the explosion in educational opportunities back home. Most Chinese universities have jumped on the bandwagon and begun offering MBA programs of their own. Many of the Western world's most prestigious universities have established programs in China as well.

One result of all this activity has been a decline in the value of an MBA degree. Most Chinese college graduates are now aware that while an MBA from a top-tier institution such as Harvard or Stanford will stand them in good stead, a degree from a lesser university may not do much to distinguish them from the pack. Rather than spending $20,000 or $30,000 a year in pursuit of that degree, many are instead opting for China-based programs.

For foreign businesses, this is a mixed blessing. It gives them a terrific pool of management talent to recruit from, but it also means that more and more Chinese firms are cutting into their competitive edge by rectifying their management deficiencies.

Once they recruit management talent, the next challenge is retention. According to the American Chamber of Commerce in China, the year 2005 saw management staffing issues displace transparency and the arbitrariness of China's regulatory environment as the number one challenge for its member companies. The nationwide turnover rate for foreign-invested business in China rose from 8.3 percent in 2001 to 14 percent in 2005. In Shanghai, the situation was considerably worse: Turnover rates rose to 14.6 percent, up from 11 percent just one year before. Companies such as General Electric have already announced plans to boost investment in employee training and retention programs for their China operations.

Despite the difficulties in finding and retaining local management talent, the payoff for a foreign company can be immense. One executive from a large British firm that runs operations all across China told me that a single expatriate manager costs his company a hundred times as much as a qualified local replacement. That ratio may seem hard to believe, but it should make more sense after you read chapter 7, where you will see that schooling for a foreign child can run above $20,000 a year, and that rental costs alone for the family of a senior expatriate executive can range as high as $8,000 per month.

On the downside, however, the same British executive told me his firm has found that wholesale replacement of foreign managers with locals has introduced a raft of new corporate governance issues. Any foreign firm in China must strike the right balance between adapting to the local environment and maintaining home-office or home-country standards. And unfortunately, the gap between the two remains very wide.

During China's headlong rush over the past quarter century toward a more market-oriented economy, the laws and standards governing corporate structure and management requirements were badly neglected. Ethical corporate conduct and shareholder rights were given very short shrift; it was not until 2001, when the China Securities Regulatory Commission (CSCR) issued its corporate governance code for listed companies, that the very term *corporate governance* even came into common usage. Upon the issuance of that code, and follow-up guidelines the following year, regulators promised to safeguard the rights of investors and shareholders, mandate transparency, and enforce board and management accountability at listed companies.

In practice, those goals have proven elusive. Most of China's listed companies were spun off from large state-owned enterprises, which usually retained a majority stake. Meanwhile, those parent enterprises were supervised by the government and by Communist party officials, whose interests often diverge sharply from those of the shareholders. The most obvious conflicts occur when political officials are more interested in bolstering employment and tax-collection rates in their jurisdiction than they are in streamlining staff in the listed subsidiaries they manage. But plenty of other management decisions can likewise be subject to political interference, including procurement decisions and operational strategy.

Things get even more dicey when it comes to delineating the assets and operations of listed entities from those of their parent. Murky lines and poor accountability mechanisms make it all too easy for funds and other assets to travel in inappropriate directions in the course of related-party transactions.

Local executives in China are gradually becoming familiar with the expectations of international corporate governance standards, but most have yet to internalize them. And the prevailing environment makes it all too easy to drift with the current into foul territory. So while a decision to pursue localization might be a shrewd step, it must be taken carefully, and constant monitoring should be maintained.

Most management gurus will tell you that in the long run, good corporate governance practices are a boon to any company's performance and profitability. Even in these still-early days of China's corporate governance reforms, there is evidence that listed Chinese companies with good CG ratings perform better.

Perhaps more importantly, markets are rewarding those companies that have gone farthest in adopting higher standards. According to a 2003 report by CLSA, the stock prices of Chinese companies that scored among the highest on corporate governance measures—such as COSCO Pacific, Zhejiang Expressway Co., Ltd., and the China National Offshore Oil Corporation—outperformed a benchmark index by 24 percent. Over the same period, stock prices of companies that scored poorly on corporate governance underperformed by 26 percent against the same benchmark.

But in the short run, more stringent home-country requirements can impose heavy burdens in cash and staff time for a foreign firm trying to match the China Price. American executives in China have had even more to complain about since the 2002 passage of the Sarbanes-Oxley Act (SOX). In addition to the related legal and accounting fees that can easily run into hundreds of thousands of dollars, SOX puts direct responsibility on executives for conduct and reporting throughout their organizations.

Given the lax standards that still prevail in China, foreign firms need to devote significant resources to monitoring their compliance, and the actions of their local staff. Many American companies, smaller ones in particular, find these burdens significant, and you should be sure to factor them into your cost projections. Unfortunately, it is a set of expenses that many of your local Chinese competitors do not need to worry about, and thus another tangible component of the China Price.

Chinese producers will soon gain a far bigger advantage when China passes planned legislation on the unification of tax rates. China's parliament, the National People's Congress, has already proposed detailed reforms, and while the details may shift before the legislation's expected passage, the outline is already clear. The proposal calls for a unified corporate tax rate of around 25 percent, a good deal lower than the 33 percent that most Chinese companies now pay, and vastly higher than the preferential rates offered to foreign firms, which can be as low as 7.5 percent.

According to researchers at Morgan Stanley, the big winners among Chinese firms will be those that have in the past ranked among tax "overpayers." These include banks, telecom firms, oil companies, and a handful of other firms in the energy, land, and heavy-industry sectors.

KEY POINTS TO REMEMBER
FROM CHAPTER 6

1. The China Price is based on a lot more than cheap labor. Plenty of other countries do have labor that is as cheap or cheaper than China, but do not pose the same competitive challenge.

2. Some elements of the China Price *are* accessible to foreign companies, allowing them to enhance their own competitiveness. But in sectors such as textiles and garments, the stars line up so well for China that it will be increasingly difficult for others to compete.

3. Western firms and Chinese firms are not competing only for market share, but also competing for access to the key HR elements of the China Price: labor and management talent.

4. Foreign firms can escape huge cost burdens by localizing the management staff of their China operations. But it needs to be done carefully, with particular attention paid to local staff's performance on corporate governance issues.

5. Compliance issues pose another huge burden on foreign companies, which have to spend large amounts of cash and devote significant amounts of staff time to the cause. Chinese firms have none of these burdens.

6. Upcoming changes in China's corporate tax code may give another big advantage to local companies. Rates are due to be unified, putting an end to the liberal tax breaks that foreign companies have enjoyed throughout most of China's reform period. Taxes will decrease for most Chinese companies and increase for most foreign ones.

7

Living Overseas,
Learning Chinese

In addition to all the stress of running a business, fighting for market share, and trying to make money, business people moving to China will also have to cope with the pressure of day-to-day living in a difficult and alien environment.

But life in China is today far less challenging for foreigners than it used to be. I confess that saying this makes me feel a bit like my father, who never passed up a chance to recount the hardships of his Depression-era childhood. As with my father's tales of hardship, though, it happens to be true: For Westerners, life in China—even in its biggest urban centers—used to involve a lot more deprivation.

In the 1980s and early 1990s, everything—from basic necessities to adequate housing or decent restaurants—was in short supply. So, too, were Western consumer items, and like most expat residents, I used to travel home to the United States with empty duffel bags to be filled with all the things I could not buy in Beijing. Coffee. Razor blades. Favorite foods. Office supplies. Diapers for the kids. And countless other items.

For some expats, the relative deprivation was all part of the romance and adventure of living in an exotic place. Others had trouble handling it, and quickly determined that life in China was not for them. Today access to creature comforts is no longer a problem for most Western residents in major Chinese cities. Just about anything is available, and for the truly homesick, a Pizza Hut or Starbucks is never too far away. Sometimes, though, even that is not enough. One case that stands out in my mind is an expatriate wife I knew who left China long before the end of her husband's posting: The final straw for her was the fact that a Big Mac in Beijing did not taste the same as it did back home in Toronto.

Even for those less fragile, life in China can impose immense stress in other ways, and there are many who fail to adapt. For business people themselves, the factors include frequent travel, regular evening business obligations, and the strain of trying to function in a place where regulations, market conditions, and just about everything else seem to change constantly.

For them, and for their families as well, added factors range from the language barrier and simple culture shock to the appalling traffic and pollution that plague most Chinese cities. It is not for nothing that most governments and multinationals still count China as a "hardship post" and provide employees with bonuses ranging from 15 to 25 percent of base salary to compensate for the challenges of living and working there.

As you saw in chapter 6, expatriate postings impose enormous costs on companies, and if your business in China is carrying a lot of expat employees, you will need to think carefully about the even greater cost of postings that fail because either employees or their families cannot handle the adjustment.

A TALE OF TWO CHINAS . . .

Without a doubt, a move to China is toughest for those who live in the country's more out-of-the-way places. Over the years, I've met many Westerners—such as a Swiss agronomist working on a start-up coffee plantation in a remote corner of Yunnan Province, and an English executive running a chemical plant in Sichuan Province—who have learned the hard way just how isolated and difficult life can be in such places.

The paucity of material comforts is, of course, a huge factor, but that is only part of the picture. Expats in postings like this are often the only Westerners for miles around, and even the ones who speak good Chinese come to miss the simple, relaxed pleasure of having someone to speak to in their own language.

Those who don't speak Chinese quickly find themselves worn down by the constant and endless struggle to understand and be understood. For these people, an English-language cable TV channel or an Internet connection can be a lifeline—if they are lucky enough to have it—and an English-language newspaper or magazine serves as a rare treat.

The strain can be relieved if these expats bring spouses or families with them. But it might just as easily be exacerbated instead. These accompanying family members can find themselves facing all the same daily aggravations, but without the focus or purpose that the employees themselves can derive from their jobs.

While the sight of a foreigner can still attract attention and curious stares anywhere in China, it has become common enough in the big cities that it no longer stops traffic. In the more far-off places, though, foreigners remain a relative rarity, and they often find themselves the object of intense and sometimes uncomfortable scrutiny. It may seem like a little thing, but over time it can become truly draining.

Remote postings are not for everyone, and regardless of whether you are preparing to send an employee to such a place or move there yourself, it is imperative that all concerned go in with a clear understanding of what to expect. The odds of success for such postings will be higher with people who have previous experience of life overseas. It is also a good idea to ensure that there are regular opportunities built into the schedule for time away. Regular visits—whether home or just to a major Chinese city—can go a long way toward relieving stress.

Paul Miller is a senior British engineer who has worked at mines and refineries in many exotic corners of the world, and in 1999 he started spending prolonged periods in the small town of Laizhou on the northern coast of Shandong

Province, working to build a state-of the-art gold refinery. By 2005, when I met him, the plant was up and running successfully, but he remained the only foreigner around. He had come to feel like a "circus act," he told me. "For the first time in my life, I knew what it felt like to be prejudiced against because of the color of my skin."

Still, as he explained, the remote location also had its upside. As the only Western investor in the area, the business enjoyed the undivided attention of local authorities. For those officials, the refining venture was a showcase project of the region, and they seemed as eager as Miller to have it succeed. Miller said he and any Western colleagues who spent time there were treated like "marquee figures."

The situation is quite different in China's larger commercial and industrial centers. There, foreign business people can enjoy the advanced support infrastructure for expat residents and the companionship of their fellow foreigners, but must at the same time compete with them for the attention and favor of local officials.

The vast majority of expatriate residents in China do end up in Beijing or Shanghai, and in these huge and modern cities the adjustment to a new lifestyle tends to be far easier. English speakers are usually not too hard to find. High-quality housing, schools, medical care, and daily necessities are widely accessible. To a lesser extent, the same is true in other major cities with high concentrations of resident foreign business people, such as Guangzhou, Shenzhen, Xiamen, or Tianjin. In fact, some of the perks of the expat lifestyle—most notably the easily affordable household help—make people worry more at the end of their postings about how they will readjust when they return home.

LEARNING CHINESE: GREEK TO YOU? MAYBE NOT.

Wherever you live and whatever your work in China, one of the most important things you can do to enhance your efficiency and your enjoyment of the experience is this: Learn at least some basic Chinese. It will require less effort than you probably imagine, and it will pay vast and lasting dividends.

There are hundreds of dialects spoken in China, some of which are mutually intelligible or very close to it, and others that are as far apart from each other as, say, English is from Dutch. As a general rule, most dialects across northern China are fairly close to one another, while the southern dialects are more varied.

But when it comes to deciding which dialect you should study, the choice is easy. Mandarin Chinese, based on the northern Beijing dialect, is the official national language, and with the exception of the most remote rural or minority regions it is universally spoken at a passable level. It is also widely spoken in Taiwan, Singapore, and, increasingly, in Hong Kong, which in 1997 returned to Chinese sovereignty.

Throughout the mainland, Mandarin is used for official business, broadcasting, and the educational system. Even in regions where people speak other dialects such as Cantonese, Sichuanese, or Shanghainese at home, Mandarin is the language of public discourse. Accents can be very heavy and hard to understand in these places, but Mandarin is what Chinese people from different regions use to speak to one another, and it is what you need to learn.

The old-time foreign China hands—the few, the brave, and the bold who one way or another got themselves to China in the early 1980s or even the late 1970s—take a particular pride in their Chinese-language skills. Almost like veterans of the military, they look back fondly on the language studies that at the time seemed a grueling ordeal but now form a common rite of passage bonding them with their fellow China hands.

Today's huge influx of expatriates into China includes plenty of younger latter-day China hands who, fresh from their own language-learning ordeals, arrive with fairly good Chinese skills in place.

But there are many who arrive with no Chinese at all. And in the main expat centers, it has—for better or worse—become far easier than it used to be to get by without it. English signs are everywhere. Among Chinese people, English is more widely spoken than ever before, especially in the offices of foreign companies where these expats usually work, and among the people they meet at foreigner-oriented housing compounds, hotels, and hangouts. In Beijing or Shanghai, it is in fact quite possible to make your way around with little or no Chinese at all. Regrettably, thousands of expats do just that.

These people are missing out on a great part of the overseas living experience. Worse still, they are shutting themselves off from vital sources of insight and information. Whether in the course of day-to-day business, getting around town, or—perhaps most importantly of all—tuning in to and understanding the environment in which you've chosen to do business, speaking Chinese at any level will be a huge plus.

For any foreigner who attains any meaningful level of Chinese competence, the rewards are substantial. Local Chinese will shower you with copious and heartfelt praise for your efforts. Meanwhile, your fellow foreigners who have yet to learn the language will openly envy you (and other Chinese-speaking foreigners are likely to quietly size up your Chinese level against their own).

Now get ready for a big surprise. I am about to share what may be the greatest dirty little secret of the China game: Learning Chinese is not so hard. Repeat that slowly to yourself and let it sink in. *Chinese is not so hard to learn.*

It is a point of national pride among Chinese people that their language is somehow uniquely difficult, and it is a common assumption among outsiders as well. And to be fair, there is a solid kernel of truth to it. The written language—which relies on ideographic characters rather than a phonetic alphabet—is in fact extremely difficult. Learning to read or write in Chinese takes a lot of time and a lot of effort, and there are no easy shortcuts. The difficulty of mastering thousands of Chinese characters is what turns formal Chinese-language courses into boot camps, and Chinese teachers into drill sergeants.

But the spoken language is another story entirely, because, with just a couple of quirky exceptions, Chinese grammar is remarkably simple. If you took high school Spanish or French, you already know that in those languages, each verb has dozens upon dozens of forms that change maddeningly according to person, tense, gender, and number. Speakers also need to modify their nouns and adjectives according to the same factors.

In languages such as Russian, German, or Greek, speakers have to grapple with all of this plus the added complication of case declensions, requiring the use of different word endings for nouns and adjectives depending on how those words function in a sentence (and then modifications of *those endings* for number and gender).

Chinese has none of this! Every verb consists of just one or two syllables, and the form never changes. To express past tense, the same simple single syllable is added after all verbs. For future tense, another single syllable is added before.

I don't mean to turn this into a grammar lesson. Nor do I intend to trivialize the undertaking. The point is simply that most Chinese grammar is far less complicated than that of the other languages you are likely to have studied before, and you should therefore not allow yourself to be intimidated by the prospect of learning Chinese. It can be done, with a lot less effort than you might think.

Easy grammar aside, there are, of course, complications. For one thing, the sounds are alien to speakers of Western languages, meaning there are no easy sound-alike words to latch onto at the beginning. So unlike a student of Spanish or German, you will not effortlessly recognize a word like *telephone* when you hear it in Chinese.

But the good news is that the overall number of sounds is limited, and Chinese words are all short, almost always consisting of only one or two syllables. With just a bit of time and effort, you can gain familiarity with the sound system.

The corresponding bad news is that in order to differentiate its relatively small number of sounds, Chinese is tonal. Any Chinese syllable must be pronounced with one of four tones, and the same syllable with different tones can mean totally different things. This can be daunting at first, because both the concept itself and the differentiated sounds of the tones are so alien to speakers of nontonal languages. But after some initial frustration at not being able to hear or produce the tones correctly, most people eventually get the hang of it and never have to think about it again.

The bottom line is this: With its alien sounds and tone system, learning spoken Chinese can be frustrating in its earliest stages, and until you figure them out the learning curve can feel steep. But once you surmount that initial hurdle, the simplicity of the grammar means you can make vast progress by merely adding new vocabulary.

If you are truly ambitious, you can try to tackle the written characters as well. But you should be prepared in this case for a more arduous experience. Learning the characters, even if you only gain the ability to recognize them passively rather than to write them yourself, can do a lot to reinforce your grasp of the spoken language. But if you prefer not to go this far, you will have no trouble making sense of pinyin, the very logical and straightforward transliteration system for Chinese that is easy for English speakers to learn and used uniformly across China (as well as in this book).

So how should you start your language-learning odyssey? Some people, especially those who have dabbled with other languages before, make very good progress on their own, splitting their efforts between a good textbook and time spent around town simply practicing. Most Chinese will be flattered by any attempt you make, and patient with any mistakes.

For those who prefer a more formal approach, there is no shortage of options. Many Chinese universities offer language programs at all levels for foreign students, although they tend not to be especially cheap or flexible. Unfortunately, if your posting brings you someplace away from the major expat centers, it may be your only option.

In most of the major cities, there are numerous specialized language schools. Prices can vary widely, but many of them can devise customized courses to suit your time constraints, level, and learning style. Among these are Beijing Mandarin School (www.beijingmandarinschool.com), Berlitz (www.berlitz.com.cn), the Bridge School (www.bridgeschoolchina.com), Executive Mandarin (www.ecbeijing.com), Frontiers (www.frontiers.com.cn), and the Hai Na Bai Wang Language Training Center (www.hnbw.cn). Some of the larger foreign companies offer in-house Chinese classes of their own for expatriate employees.

Private tutors are also easily found through word of mouth, message boards at foreigner hangouts, and classified ads in the expat-oriented publications that have proliferated in recent years. Rates can be surprisingly affordable, running as low as 100 RMB ($12) per hour for private lessons in your own home or office.

HOUSING

If you came to China twenty years ago, your choice of housing would have been depressingly simple. If you were a diplomat, you would have been required to live either inside your embassy compound or in one of several specially built (and tightly guarded) diplomatic apartment complexes. And if you were in business, your choice would have boiled down to the handful of hotels that were authorized to accept foreigners. As my wife, Roberta, among other foreign China pioneers, can attest, living for years on end in a standard hotel room— with shoddy plumbing, no kitchen, and dim lighting—took quite a lot of getting used to.

Today, though, your choices are wide open. Regulations vary somewhat by locality, but in most of China they have been eased over the years to the point that foreigners are now allowed to buy or rent just about anywhere they want, including local Chinese housing. New buildings are coming online all the time, where decent but simple apartments can be had for just a few hundred dollars a month. Apartments at these prices may even be furnished and include foreign cable television channels.

For foreigners brought to China by large companies, the employment contract typically includes a housing stipend that will allow you to live in more luxurious single-family detached houses. In China's biggest cities, you can choose from the dozens of gated compounds that have sprung up in the suburban outskirts to cater to the foreign influx. The largest of these compounds, often located near the most popular international schools, consists of hundreds of cookie-cutter houses that rent from a few thousand dollars to as much as $8,000 per month. At this level, the deal usually includes a garage, yard, and access to an on-site health club and pool.

The vast majority of corporate expats live in places like this. It is a choice that involves a huge trade-off, for each of these compounds is half enclave and half ghetto, offering comfort and convenience on the one hand, but a strange brand of segregation on the other. Residents can all too easily fall back on the easy familiarity of their isolated community of fellow foreigners and miss the opportunity to connect with the China that lies just beyond the gates of their compound.

Finding Housing

The steady influx of foreigners into China has fed a genuine real estate boom at the expat-oriented high end of the housing market. In a 2006 report, international property consultancy Jones Lang LaSalle predicted at least three more years of continued strong growth in Beijing's luxury home rental market. About seventy-five hundred new luxury units came online in 2005 in Beijing alone, and similarly large increases are expected in coming years. The report attributed this growth to demand that will be generated both by the upcoming 2008

Beijing Olympics and by the continued expansion by multinationals of their China operations.

Not only will these companies continue to bring in expats in need of high-end housing, but the multinationals are also working hard to localize their China workforces. This trend means they are hiring more local employees, usually Western-educated, at salaries that allow them to live in these same properties. In addition to keeping the market strong, this trend is already helping to make the compounds less segregated.

When it comes to finding the right housing, companies such as Jones Lang LaSalle play a key role, acting as agents. Other such companies include CB Richard Ellis, Colliers International, and Joanna Real Estate. Typically, they work together with your employer to find a place that matches your preferences and your budget, though most of them also work with individuals. In some cases, though, companies already hold long-term leases on a number of units in a particular compound, meaning their employees may have little choice in the matter.

Though they are in the minority, some foreigners know they will be in China long enough to justify a purchase rather than a rental. If properly structured, a deal like this can allow employees to apply their housing allowances to the purchase of their own homes. Under today's more liberal regulations, foreigners are allowed to own property just about anywhere. They can also access mortgages from Chinese banks.

But such deals are not without risk. For one thing, Chinese law still prohibits outright ownership of land, and so what buyers actually obtain are land-use rights that eventually expire, typically after seventy years. The law is not always clear as to what exactly happens to property at the end of such a period, and while it is unlikely that all rights to the property would be forfeited, there is considerable uncertainty as to what it would take to renew them.

Another danger comes from the freewheeling nature of the Chinese real estate sector. Some of China's most sensational scandals in recent years have involved unscrupulous developers who have sold property to which they did not have full legal title. Anyone contemplating a real estate purchase in China must therefore tread carefully, working with local legal help to verify as far as possible the validity of any developer's claim to title.

DRIVING IN CHINA

Among the first questions foreigners ask upon visiting me in China is whether I drive—and upon hearing that I do, how I can stand it. In a way I am lucky, because the mind-boggling chaos on display today on Chinese roads wasn't so bad when I began driving here in 1989. Instead, it has built up gradually around me, allowing me to get used to it. But anyone who arrives in China today and is thinking of taking to the roads needs to be prepared for an exasperating experience.

You've already read in chapter 1 about the many ways "car culture" has transformed both China's landscape and its economy. When I first arrived, bicycles were everywhere and private cars were the almost exclusive preserve of foreign residents. Chinese officials of a certain rank had cars at their disposal, too, but they never drove themselves. Instead, they had chauffeurs, and just about anyone in China who drove a motor vehicle at that time did so professionally.

In the cities at that time, driving was already something of a challenge, but mostly because of the densely packed crowds of bicycles and pedestrians, and the varied sprinkling of trucks, animal carts, and buses. The greatest hazards were posed by pedestrians, the vast majority of whom had never driven themselves and thus had not the slightest understanding of how much time and space a car needs to stop. But even with that, it did not take long to discern a certain rhythm to it all, and it was always easy enough to slip into the flow.

Traffic jams, meanwhile, were unheard of, and parking was simply not an issue. It was something of a delight to drive in one of the world's major capitals without giving a thought to rush-hour traffic patterns, then park at will without paying a cent.

Things began to change in the mid-1990s as hordes of new cars and new drivers first came onto the scene. The pace has only accelerated, with the number of cars on the streets of Beijing alone having doubled in the past five years to surpass 3 million. That figure is projected to increase by a further 40 percent by 2008.

Today the streets of Beijing remind me of nothing so much as an American high school parking lot: full of newly licensed car owners, all brimming with enthusiasm and eager to show off their new status symbols, but sorely lacking mastery of even the most basic driving skills.

Lacking also is any sense of courtesy or decorum. The Chinese rules of the road appear instead to mimic the Chinese rules of lining up at a train station ticket window: Squeeze in, seize ground, and never yield an inch to anyone. Laws, lights, lane markers—not to mention the dictates of basic common sense—are all taken as mere suggestions. If there is no physical barrier preventing it (or policeman there to fine them for it), Chinese drivers will brazenly cut in wherever they can. It is a distressingly common sight to see drivers slip into the oncoming traffic lane, or come at you the wrong way on highway exit and entrance ramps.

Only when I return to the relative sanity of driving in America (even in such notoriously hectic driving environments as Boston, Manhattan, or South Florida) do I come to appreciate how wild things in China really are. Congestion and even rudeness are common enough on American roads, to be sure. The difference in China is the unpredictability of it all. Cars may come at you from any direction at any time. Or they may simply stop instead. All too often, Chinese drivers (whose navigational skills are usually no better than their driving) will come to a full stop in the middle of a three-lane highway in order to read signs, check maps, and figure out where to go. People often don't bother to use directional signals, as if tipping you off to their next move might give you some kind of unfair advantage. Nor has anyone yet caught on to the idea that slower traffic should keep to one side. Instead, most drivers seem to choose their lanes at random.

Pedestrians are no better, and in a way it's hard to blame them. Streets are marked with crosswalks, but drivers have no obligation to stop. (In fact, you will surprise them if you do. I long ago gave up yielding to pedestrians because they usually freeze up, apparently unable to believe that I would actually let them go.) City intersections all allow right turns on red; drivers are not even required to stop first, and you will in fact earn a contemptuous blast of the horn from the car behind if you do. So even when they have a green light with them, pedestrians have an awful time trying to cross, and to make up for it, they feel perfectly free to dash across against a red light if they think they can make it.

Other challenges are posed by poor signage and the poor design of many Chinese roads. Like the nation's drivers, Chinese road engineers and urban planners are still learning by doing. On city streets and interprovince highway alike, planning and design standards are lacking. This, too, is something I appreciate more fully upon returning to the United States and seeing how much a well-designed highway entrance ramp or an optimally programmed set of traffic lights can do to facilitate the flow of traffic.

Quality is improving with each new road that gets built, and planners are experimenting freely to overhaul existing intersections that don't work well. Separate turn lanes and better sequencing of traffic lights are being introduced, but keeping up with the steadily increasing number of vehicles remains a challenge. (And I am still waiting for someone in the Beijing city government to figure out that sending street sweepers out at rush hour causes more problems than it's worth.)

With all this, it is not surprising that accidents are common. China now records about one hundred thousand traffic fatalities each year, and the figure is rising 10 percent annually, according to the World Health Organization. Those numbers are not helped by the fact that most people still scorn seat belts and tend to keep young children on their laps, unbelted, in the front seat.

The good news is that in the congested cities, where you are likely to do most of your driving, the traffic usually moves so slowly that the fender benders are seldom serious. The bad news is that drivers involved in any collision are supposed to leave their cars in place until police arrive, so the frequency of accidents, even minor ones, is just one more of the many factors contributing to the traffic problems in China's cities. My own ride to work is only about eight miles, but it usually takes me between thirty and forty minutes, and it is a rare day indeed when I don't encounter a tie-up caused by a minor accident.

Unfortunately, your problems are not over once you finally get where you're going. Parking has become another major hassle. Newer buildings are now designed with underground parking facilities, but many older buildings went up at a time when no one thought much about it.

Not surprisingly in the market economy that China has become, the scarcity of parking has driven prices up. To someone moving from a major American city, the rates may seem laughably low, but they are a significant sum by Chinese standards. Renting a dedicated spot at a downtown office or apartment building can cost around 400 yuan ($50) per month. Hourly rates for streetside parking range from 2 to 5 yuan (25 to 60 cents) an hour. Rates in the overcrowded parking lots of top hotels sometimes run as high as 10 yuan ($1.25) per hour.

Add it all up—the poor skills and brazen rudeness of drivers, the haphazard road design, and the increasingly heavy volume—and the sad result is nasty stop-and-go traffic in most Chinese cities during most hours of the day. This state of affairs is certainly not unique among the world's great cities, but it does mark a big change from the way things used to be just ten or fifteen years ago, and it definitely ranks as a major quality-of-life issue for anyone contemplating a move to China.

If despite all this you are still interested in joining the fray, you will have to get a local driver's license. Those traveling on tourist or visitor's visas are not allowed to drive, but once you get the work visa and residence permit you need to live in China, you are eligible to apply for a Chinese license.

In this regard, too, I was lucky, arriving in China at a time when the only requirements were the residence permit, a valid home-country license, and a simple test of eyesight and hearing. Rules vary from place to place, but in most cities foreign drivers are now required to pass both a written test (in English) and a practical test on a closed course.

If, on the other hand, the drama and frustration of driving in this environment are all too much for you, there are ways around it. Public transport is being improved in most big cities and can be an option for those who don't mind crowds (and who have enough Chinese to find their way around). Better still are taxis, which are plentiful and reasonably priced. Still, they don't solve the traffic problem for you.

Most taxi drivers will cheerfully put out their cigarettes and turn down the radio if you ask them to, but they are not likely to perform any heroics to get you to your meeting on time. In fact, they may be among the most conservative drivers on the road, since they cannot risk their livelihoods by accumulating points on their licenses for violations.

The best solution of all is a full-time driver. Many companies provide this perk for senior expatriate staff, and it is less expensive than you might imagine. Depending on the vehicle, the total cost of a car and a full-time driver should range from $600 to $1,000 per month. Many executives find it money well spent, as it allows them to sit in the backseat making good use of the time they would otherwise lose to traffic jams and parking hassles. Beyond that, a good driver can also serve as an invaluable assistant, running banking and other errands. Like housekeepers, personal drivers are one of the things people miss most after leaving China.

POLLUTION

Another consequence of the Chinese car boom is worsening air pollution in most cities. Things were already bad enough before the emergence of cars, thanks to the potent mix of pollutants produced by lightly regulated Chinese industry and the widespread use of inefficient coal stoves for household heating and cooking.

With the addition of exhaust emissions from China's burgeoning motor vehicle fleet, the noxious airborne stew is only growing thicker. According to a World Bank study of global air quality, sixteen of the world's twenty most polluted cities are in China. The nation's own State Environmental Protection Administration has reported that 400 out of China's 661 cities consistently fail to meet minimally acceptable air-quality standards. If you want to track the grim facts yourself, SEPA maintains a Web site with daily updates on air-quality conditions in more than eighty Chinese cities: www.zhb.gov.cn/english/air-list.php3.

Western experts have doubts about the standards and methodology used for SEPA's measurements. But if you check the site on a regular basis, you will find that Beijing consistently ranks among the very worst, and on this point Western experts tend to agree. A 2005 report by the European Space Agency determined that the air in Beijing and its neighboring provinces has the world's highest concentration of nitrogen dioxide. As it prepares to host the 2008 Summer Olympics, Beijing has been scrambling to improve its air, but so far the results have been disappointing. The city has consistently failed to meet its own goals for the monthly number of "blue sky days," and to avoid the embarrassment of having air unfit for athletes to breathe, officials will likely have to resort to draconian restrictions on car traffic and industrial operations in the weeks before the games.

Of all the quality-of-life issues raised by a move to China, this may be the most troublesome. It is distressing enough on a day-to-day basis. Smog, sandstorms, itchy eyes, and scratchy throats are all part of everyday life. Schools frequently have to keep children indoors and cancel athletic events when the air is especially bad. And it can be an emotional drain when you realize you haven't actually seen the sun or a blue sky for weeks at a time.

It is less pleasant still to contemplate the long-term effects. Chinese researchers blame air pollution for four hundred thousand annual premature deaths. Apart from the air quality, there are other environmental hazards. About 70 percent of China's lakes and rivers are polluted, making bottled water a wise choice anywhere in the country. At least one-third of China is regularly visited by acid rain. Pesticides and other agricultural chemicals are also poorly regulated and badly overused.

Despite the growing recognition at all levels of the government of how serious these problems are, China will have a hard time turning the tide. The country is already the world's second largest source of greenhouse gas emissions and is projected to eventually surpass the United States for the top spot. One senior Chinese environmental official warned in 2005 that pollution levels nationwide could be expected to quadruple within fifteen years if China were to maintain its current growth rates in energy consumption and car ownership.

As I write this on yet another of Beijing's many "bad air days," I find it hard to imagine how any more grime could possibly be squeezed into the air. But most residents, foreign and local alike, learn to live with it and hope for the best. Some people are disappointed to find upon arriving in China that their cherished morning run does more harm than good. In homes and offices, most people use air purifiers (although changing the filters can be a rather sobering exercise).

For anyone contemplating a move to a major Chinese city, the issue has to be taken into account. And the sad fact is that if you or anyone in your family suffers from asthma or other respiratory problems, you probably ought to think twice about relocating to any major Chinese city.

HEALTH CARE

Whether it's air pollution or something else that causes medical problems for you, access to health care is another important consideration for anyone contemplating a move to China. Yet again, location makes all the difference. If you are unfortunate enough to need medical care in a rural part of China, you will probably be in for a harrowing experience. Doctors, money, and facilities are stretched very thin across the Chinese countryside, and you cannot be assured of getting the help you need. It is worth keeping in mind that for frail, elderly, or chronically sick travelers, rural China can be a risky place to spend time.

Things are better in any large or medium-size Chinese city. There you can be sure to find an adequately equipped major hospital staffed by competent professionals who are fully trained in standard Western medicine. Unfortunately, you can also be sure to find it dreadfully overcrowded and a lot dirtier than you'd like. And what you may *not* find is English-speaking staff. If you do seek medical care in places like this, you will have to put up with a lot of frustration, especially if you don't speak Chinese. And you are likely to be put off by the standards of hygiene. But as a "foreign guest," you will be given whatever special treatment the hospital can muster, including a private room, if possible, and access to senior staff. In the end, you stand a fair chance of receiving competent care.

Only in the largest cities will you have an easy time finding top-notch care in a comfortable and clean environment. Most of China's elite hospitals run special wards that cater to foreigners (and senior Chinese officials). Their doctors are the best in the nation, many of whom have studied and practiced medicine in the West. English is widely spoken, equipment is state of the art, and hygiene is usually passable. Just be sure to bring cash, because they are unlikely to accept either credit cards or insurance.

In the largest cities, you can also choose from a wide range of foreign clinics and hospitals. Most are staffed with at least some Western doctors, and the best are run to the very highest international standards. Many provide basic outpatient treatment, pediatric services, dentistry, and prenatal care. They can also help transfer more serious cases to full-service local hospitals, or arrange medical evacuations out of the country. Other foreign providers offer more comprehensive inpatient services, including surgery, obstetrics, and intensive care. Prices run high at these places, but many will accept your home-country insurance. Unlike local hospitals, they will also accept credit cards.

In Beijing and Shanghai, the most comprehensive services are offered at the United Family Hospital facilities. (I must repeat here that these facilities are built and operated by

Chindex International, the company run by my wife. Despite my obvious bias, I maintain in good faith that the standards and services there are first-rate, and I feel it is preferable to provide this information with full disclosure rather than exclude it because of concerns about a potential conflict of interest.) Locations and contact information are available at www.unitedfamilyhospitals.com.

Other top-tier options in Beijing include the Bayley & Jackson Medical Center (www.bjhealthcare.com); the International Medical Center (www.imcclinics.com); and the Hong Kong International Medical Clinic, Beijing (www.hkclinic.com/en/index.asp).

International SOS (www.internationalsos.com) manages clinics in Beijing as well as Tianjin, Nanjing, and other Chinese cities. Another provider with coverage in major Chinese cities is Global Doctor (www.eglobaldoctor.com). Among the major Chinese hospitals in Beijing that cater to foreigners are Peking Union Medical College Hospital and the Sino-Japanese Friendship Hospital.

In Shanghai, options include the World Link Medical & Dental Centers (www.worldlink-shanghai.com); the Shanghai East International Medical Center (www.seimc.com.cn); and the local HuaShan Hospital.

SCHOOLS

The "right" kind of school is, of course, a highly subjective and personal matter, and as they would anywhere else, parents need to think carefully about what kind of environment and learning styles are best suited for their kids. Fortunately, China's main cities now offer a wealth of choices. As with housing, recent years have seen an explosion in the number of schooling options for foreign families to choose from in major Chinese cities. They range from the many local Chinese schools that are now authorized to accept foreign students to huge foreigner-only schools catering to the kids of diplomats, journalists, and employees of multinational corporations. The right choice on schooling is often key to a successful posting, and care should be taken in making it.

Some of the schools cater mainly to specific nationalities but also accept students from elsewhere. In Beijing, these include the Russian, French, Swedish, Japanese, and Pakistani schools, operated by the embassies or expat communities from those countries. Other schools are incredibly diverse, providing a stimulating mix of teachers and students from all over the world. In terms of facilities, they range from the simple to the state of the art. Most can be relied on to have a qualified and committed teaching staff, but some of the smaller or more recently established schools have yet to prove themselves.

The best ones, however, are extremely expensive, posing a tremendous burden on the many companies that cover school fees for their employees, and a real challenge for employees who have to pay for them personally.

China's oldest and largest Western school is the International School of Beijing (ISB), where annual fees range from $16,500 for kindergarten to $21,300 for high school. With eighteen hundred students, it is housed in a huge, new state-of-the-art building in the northeast corner of Beijing, close to the biggest concentration of expat housing developments. Instruction is in English, and teachers come from countries all across the English-speaking world, including not only the United States but also Canada, Australia, New Zealand, Ireland, and Britain.

The student body is even more diverse, with kids from more than fifty countries. Americans and Europeans are well represented, and the South Korean contingent is expanding quickly, reflecting the booming trade ties between China and South Korea. The curriculum is modeled on American standards; graduates routinely win placements in the world's top universities.

ISB and other top international schools offer rich programs teaching Chinese as a second language. With the ample immersion opportunities afforded by living in China, and the natural capacity of young children to absorb new languages, many foreign kids quickly achieve impressive levels of fluency in Chinese. This is a tremendous fringe benefit to any family posted in China, and with the certainty that Chinese will continue to gain importance around the world in the future, many families make efforts to maintain and reinforce their children's Chinese-language skills after returning home.

Some families go farther, choosing to put their kids into local Chinese-language schools. It is a decision to be weighed carefully. One advantage is the cost, and for families who are footing the bill themselves, it may be the only feasible option. Fees at a local school can be as low as $750 per year.

But the cost advantage needs to be weighed against the difficulty newly arrived children are bound to experience in the early stages. Although most kids, especially younger ones, quickly get up to speed on their Chinese, many others struggle at first, and parents need to think carefully about whether their kids are more likely to thrive or wilt in the face of that kind of challenge.

Another consideration is the overall quality of education. It is easy enough to supplement and compensate for the rather tendentious leanings of the Chinese curriculum on subjects such as history and current affairs. But remember that the Chinese educational system is also heavily geared toward rote learning, discipline, and conformity. Little attention is paid to fostering creativity, individuality, or free thinking, and Western kids coming out of Chinese schools can be poorly prepared for reentry into the Western academic environment, where these priorities are reversed.

For foreign kids who plan to spend only a year or two in China, local schools may be worthwhile as a stimulating and eye-opening option that truly enriches their overall experience of the country and the culture. But for children who expect to receive a major portion of their education in China before entering college back home, local schooling can leave them unprepared, and it may not be a wise choice.

Families also need to think carefully about a move to China if they have children with any sort of special learning needs. Even at the very best of the international schools, counseling and special education resources are extremely thin. Kids with emotional or developmental problems simply cannot count on getting the extra support they need to succeed. Admissions departments at these schools are quite frank about their shortcomings in this area, and generally do a good job of realistically outlining the levels of support they can provide.

Information about some of Beijing's major foreign schools is available at www.beijing.alloexpat.com. For a good listing of Shanghai schools, visit www.easyexpat.com.

CRIME AND SAFETY

Another myth that China used to cultivate (and that a lot of foreigners used to buy) is that crime was virtually unknown during the glorious heyday of socialism. I always found that hard to square with the fact that just about every building—including the old ones built back in that so-called heyday—featured iron bars on all the ground-floor windows. Obviously, a lot of people were worried about keeping out the bad guys.

Today there is no doubt that China, like just about any other place in the world, has its fair share of crime. In recent years especially, reforms and rapid growth have created impressive new levels of wealth, but they have also created great disparities. The proximity of haves and have-nots, coupled with the expectations spawned by the new consumer culture, have inevitably led to an increase in crime.

Because they are typically far wealthier than the average local, foreigners stand out as obvious potential targets. But at the same time, they enjoy a degree of insulation. Local thieves well know that prosecution for any crime involving a foreign victim would carry with it a whole new level of complexity and severity, and many of them prefer to avoid the added risk.

Still, it is no longer safe to say, as it once was, that crime against foreigners is unknown. Pickpockets are a constant menace, and forcible muggings are no longer unheard of. Isolated incidents of sexual assault against foreign victims have been reported in recent years, as have murders.

Most of the foreigner-oriented housing compounds have good security, with closed-circuit cameras, ubiquitous guards patrolling the grounds, and controlled access at their gates. Even at these places, however, the safety record is not perfect. A German auto executive's family of four was brutally stabbed to death in their villa house in the city of Nanjing in 2000, and in 2006 the wife of an American businessman was stabbed to death in her home in one of Beijing's premier gated housing compounds for expats. Events like these show that the ordinary precautions of city living are obviously in order, but such incidents are in fact quite rare, and overall crime is not a major concern. In addition, since gun ownership is not at all common in China, the incidence of gun-related crime is extremely low.

Apart from crime, foreigners in China should also be wary of getting stuck in the middle of angry crowds. In the case of any sort of altercation, a crowd is sure to gather. If one of the participants is foreign, the crowd is likely to quickly take sides and can just as quickly turn ugly. Whether over a minor car crash or a minor insult, these situations can be dangerous. The best advice is to keep calm, keep smiling, and, if possible, keep moving.

Political events have also inspired violent mob behavior in China. Often the targets are the Japanese, who since World War II have been intensely disliked throughout China. In August 2004, ugly riots followed China's loss to Japan at the Asia Cup soccer final in Beijing. In another outburst the following year, angry mobs in Beijing and Shanghai broke windows at Japanese businesses, stoned the Japanese embassy, and burned Japanese cars.

Americans have also been targets, most notably in spring 1999 when, during the war in Yugoslavia, US forces bombed the Chinese embassy in Belgrade and killed three Chinese nationals. For the following four days, thousands of angry Chinese demonstrated in Beijing's diplomatic quarter, roughing up Americans in the streets and pummeling the US embassy with bricks, garbage, pavement stones, and paint bombs. I had already been living in Beijing for ten years at that point, and never had the feeling that such virulent anti-American sentiment lay so close to the surface and could be so readily activated. I didn't resort to the tactic adopted by other Americans during that period—that is, claiming to be Canadian. At the same time, I have never forgotten the potential for these situations to get ugly.

SHOPPING

Given the enthusiasm with which the world imports goods from China, it should come as no surprise to learn that the country is a shopper's paradise. From clothing to electrical appliances and everything in between, local stores have abundant supplies of consumer goods at fairly reasonable prices.

In chapter 4, you read about the Chinese housing reforms that—among other things—were aimed at kick-starting economic activity in the home improvement sector. If you move to China, you can consider yourself the lucky beneficiary of those reforms. Furniture and home improvement stores are everywhere, offering either Western-style or traditional Chinese-style furniture in all price ranges, as well as top-notch floorings, fabrics, and other materials.

Antiques lovers will never run out of flea-market stalls to visit, and clothes hounds can buy good-quality silk or cashmere garments at excellent prices at any of the markets scattered throughout most Chinese cities. Raw cloth and expert tailors are both available at low cost, too, making custom clothing a very reasonable option.

In market stalls, negotiating is a must, since vendors will typically quote outrageously high prices on the off chance you might say yes. A good rule of thumb is to counter an initial quote by offering a third as much, and then negotiate your way to half the originally quoted price. If you pay more than that, you are probably giving in too soon.

Open haggling is less welcome in larger stores, but there is nothing wrong with a single, polite attempt to ask whether a discount is available. The answer could go either way.

Many foreigners in China tread on ethical thin ice by indulging in the easy availability of all the knockoff products and counterfeit goods you read about in chapter 2. There is no small irony in the fact that many expats, working for companies that endlessly lobby China for better IPR protection, spend their weekends scouring Chinese market stalls for pirated DVDs, knockoff Nikes, and fake North Face jackets.

When it comes to everyday household shopping, local supermarket chains in most cities carry a good range of basic groceries and an ever-increasing volume of imported packaged products. This is a tremendous improvement over my earliest days in China, when fresh milk was available only a couple of days a week and in limited quantities at the state-run, foreigner-only Friendship Store in Beijing's diplomatic district.

For the widest selection of familiar brands and products, expats in major Chinese cities flock to the specialty shops opened by enterprising locals who in recent years have figured out what Westerners like, and how to import it. The selection of products available at these places is enough to make you feel guilty about getting that hardship bonus. (Then again the prices, ranging from one and a half to two times what you might pay at home for the same products, are enough to help you get over it.) There are European cheeses, obscure spices, and gourmet Belgian ales. Familiar brands of breakfast cereals, sauces, and prepared foods fill the shelves, and imported frozen foods are increasingly making their way to the freezers in these stores. If you have a craving for a Snapple, a can of Campbell's soup, or a box of taco shells, you can probably find it, at least in Beijing or Shanghai.

The selection of personal care items is somewhat more limited. Whether it's deodorant, toothpaste, shampoo, or diapers, you can always count on finding something, but not necessarily your favorite brand. Many foreigners with strong preferences still find it necessary to stock up on these items during their home visits.

If all else fails, the shopping option of last resort is the Internet, but it can be a hit-or-miss proposition, depending on the sensibilities of Chinese customs. Many online retailers, including Amazon.com, will deliver to China, and very often customs allows such shipments to enter the country without formalities. Sometimes, however, they do choose to inspect, and they can either charge prohibitive import duties or, in the case of books or other materials they find objectionable, simply confiscate the goods.

KEY POINTS TO REMEMBER
FROM CHAPTER 7

1. Living in China involves a great deal of stress and deprivation, especially for foreigners living anywhere outside of the main cities. It is less stressful than it used to be, but even so, it's not for everybody. All concerned—employers, employees, and family members—need to be clear about the magnitude of the challenge.

2. The dirty little secret is out! *Spoken Chinese isn't so hard to learn.* It can take a while to get comfortable with the alien sounds and to learn how to use tones. But once these initial hurdles are crossed, you'll find

that the grammar is simple, allowing for fast and easy progress. It will enhance your enjoyment of China and your effectiveness in your work—and is well worth the effort.

3. Housing options in China are now wide open, ranging from cheap local apartments to luxury villas in expat compounds, where comfort and convenience come at the expense of cutting yourself off from the "real China." Buying is even an option, and one that may make sense for long-termers.

4. Resident foreigners are allowed to drive in China, but it can be a nerve-racking experience and is not for the fainthearted. Bad roads, bad signage, bad traffic, and above all bad local drivers combine to make every trip an adventure. Your time can be better spent sitting in the backseat with your laptop and your cell phone while your driver handles the hassles.

5. Pollution is quite severe in most Chinese cities. Beijing's air is especially bad, but pollution is a major quality-of-life issue in just about all cities here. People with asthma or other respiratory problems will have a very difficult time living in China.

6. Adequate health care can be found in most Chinese cities, although crowds and hygiene standards are likely to be off-putting. Foreign providers and top Chinese hospitals offer excellent health care services in the largest cities. Many foreign insurance policies will cover costs in China, but check with your provider first. Health care services in the countryside are

threadbare, and anyone with chronic health problems should not plan on spending a lot of time there.

7. Schools of all kinds are now available, ranging from top-notch international schools costing more than $20,000 a year to local Chinese institutions that cost as little as $750. Some kids thrive on the challenge of adjusting to Chinese schools, but others wilt, and the decision needs to be weighed carefully. Even the best schools, however, lack adequate resources for special learning needs.

8. Apart from the hazards of pollution and traffic, China is a relatively safe place. It is not crime-free, but it is far from crime-ridden. Foreigners have been victimized in occasional incidents, but in general crime is not a major issue. Angry crowds *can* pose a threat, however.

9. China offers endless opportunities for shopping enthusiasts. Clothes, furniture, antiques, and a million other products are widely available at department stores and market stalls in any Chinese city. Groceries and daily necessities are also widely available at specialty stores. If your favorite brand is important to you, you may need to bring it from home, but in most product categories you can count on finding what you need.

8

Pitfalls to Avoid

By now, you should have a good appreciation of the many
and varied opportunities China's booming economy presents
to Western companies. But you have also seen how pitfalls
both large and small lurk at every step on the path to success.
The aim of this chapter is to highlight some of the most dangerous ones, and to offer the guidance you will need to chart
a course around them.

Many have been touched on in previous chapters, such as
the easy tendency to neglect your relationships with local officials, or the potential for misunderstanding the interests and
objectives of your local partners. These issues bear repeating here, because a failure to handle them properly can cause
you huge problems. But the remedies in these cases are fairly
straightforward. By doing your homework ahead of time, you
can gain a fairly solid understanding of what your partners

and counterparts are expecting. And keeping up your relationships with regulators is merely a matter of remembering that you need to, then scheduling the time to do it. So we might as well start instead with one of the thorniest pitfalls of all.

CORRUPTION

By the common consensus of the most experienced foreign business people in China, international experts, and even China's own top officials, corruption is right near the top of the list of China's problems. And unfortunately, it has been for many years. In February 2006, Chinese Prime Minister Wen Jiabao said it as plainly as he could: "Bribery has poisoned the ethos of administrative, industrial and social practices and has become a plague."

That's quite an eye-catching quote, but it's also nothing new. Upon seeing it, I immediately thought back to the 1990s, when senior leaders called corruption in China a "cancer," and then-President Jiang Zemin said that solving the problem was "a matter of life and death for the party and the state." Even then, though, the news articles I wrote about it emphasized that such dire warnings were themselves nothing but tired retreads of previous statements.

For the government, of course, the impact of corruption on foreign business is only one of many worrying aspects of the problem. More importantly, in the view of the leadership, the corrupt behavior of officials at all levels inhibits the ability of the government to implement its laws and policies; worse, it rankles badly across all sectors of Chinese society. The prolonged failure of the government to curb official corruption is one of the leading complaints among ordinary Chinese, and it is no exaggeration to say it is one of their leading reasons for questioning the legitimacy of their leaders. The government is undoubtedly right in viewing corruption as a serious threat to its long-term rule.

For any foreigner doing business in China, meanwhile, corruption is likely to emerge as one of the most nettlesome challenges. There is no foolproof way to handle it, but you will be better equipped if you know what to expect, and decide in advance how to respond. Corruption—in its worst forms, anyway—can often be resisted. The key is steadfastness.

While the domestic political implications of the corruption issue cause it greater concern, the Chinese government is fully aware that the issue also damages China's international reputation as a business destination. And the nation has taken a wide variety of measures aimed at curbing corruption, but none seem to make much of a difference. In recent years, for example, the government has tried far-reaching reforms in official procurement policies. Instead of having government departments negotiate directly with suppliers on high-value contracts, an elaborate system of regulated tender bidding has been established. A seemingly well-advised initiative, it has nevertheless failed to produce drastic improvements.

Instead (and perhaps predictably), the reforms have added new nodes of decision making and additional layers of bureaucrats to the business of government procurement. So now, in addition to the officials who are making purchasing decisions, there are other officials managing the tender process. And they have so far proved just as susceptible to the temptation to abuse their positions.

The authorities also periodically launch high-profile crackdowns on corrupt officials. The crackdowns gain a lot of attention in the state-run media, and they have in fact netted plenty of wrongdoers over the years. Between 2004 and 2006 alone, China claimed to have sent fifty thousand corrupt officials to prison. Executions for such crimes are not at all uncommon.

But the deterrent effects seem fleeting at best. Officials who have access to state funds continue to embezzle and divert with reckless abandon. Officials who have access to land or other state-owned assets take them as their own, and those who manage the budgets of large government projects routinely line their pockets. Chinese press reports carry a steady stream of news on accounting scams, sweetheart bank loans, nepotism, and every other imaginable kind of fraud and swindle. In the most high-profile cases in over a decade, the highest-ranking official in Shanghai, Party Secretary Chen Liangyu, was removed from office in September 2006 amid accusations of vast corruption involving tens of millions of dollars' worth of city pension funds.

In its comprehensive 2005 worldwide survey on perceptions of corruption, Transparency International, a Berlin-based civil society organization, ranked 159 countries. It should come as little surprise to anyone that nations such as Finland, New Zealand, and Singapore ranked among the world's cleanest.

But as frank as China has been about its own corruption issues, it cannot have been pleased to see itself ranked below countries like Laos, Syria, and Panama. (The greatest consolation probably lies in the fact that India scored even worse, by a significant margin.)

In September 2006, China's National Audit Office investigated forty-two different central government ministries and institutions and found serious financial misconduct in every one.

For foreign businesses, one result of all this murky dealing is that they can easily find themselves up against rivals whose shenanigans afford them illicit but immensely valuable competitive advantages.

An even greater menace, though, comes when officials who have the power to make or break your business come looking for bribes. Such come-ons can range from subtle to brazen to anything in between. And while the temptation to play along can be great, it should be resisted. The legal and ethical factors are obvious enough. But even in purely amoral tactical terms, caving in to a would-be bribe taker is not a shrewd move.

In an apt comparison, a foreign lawyer with many years of China experience once told me that agreeing to bribery can be like agreeing to drink with your dinner host. At a typical Chinese banquet, a gregarious host is likely to ask you to take part in a round of toasts and join the rest of the table in throwing back glass after glass of hundred-proof Chinese grain liquor. In terms of both its taste and its kick, this is very harsh stuff, and many Westerners simply do not like it. Many others, of course, do not—or cannot—drink at all.

Whatever your reasons, you will usually have a very hard time holding your ground if you try to decline the offer. You will be told it is a matter of Chinese manners. And you will probably be asked to have just one small glass as a sign of your sincerity, and for the sake of your mutual friendship. "Go ahead," goes the pitch. "It may not be your habit, but this is how things are done here in China." One thing is certain, though: If you give in at that point, your glass will promptly be refilled and the pressure to keep going will just increase.

The only reliable way to stay out of trouble, my lawyer friend wisely advised, is never to start. You can politely tell your host you are allergic to spirits and suggest a toast with beer or even soft drinks instead. The pressure is likely to continue for a while longer anyway, and you may sense an unpleasant change in the mood. But the key is to hold firm. Because if you give in just once, you will have merely proved that your initial stand was not so steadfast after all, and subsequent refusals will become that much more difficult for you.

Whether it is an aggressive invitation to drink when you don't care to, or a naked request for a bribe you don't want to pay, the dynamic remains very much the same. If you cave in, you may be headed for a nasty headache and the possibility of severe embarrassment.

In the case of a bribe request, there is a real chance that your refusal will jeopardize a deal, especially if you have competitors who are prepared to pay up. If so, though, you need to ask yourself several key questions. Is the deal worth the legal risks and the potential damage to your company's international reputation? What happens when your official gets swept up in China's next great corruption crackdown? And when all is said and done, can you really trust this type of person not to turn around later and stab you in the back?

Remember also that in many cases, would-be bribe takers ask as a shot-in-the-dark gambit, merely because they know they can, and because they know there is just a chance you might agree. Plenty of Western executives have resisted bribery attempts with no lasting consequences. It can be especially useful for American companies to refer to the strict constraints of American laws. Your Chinese counterparts may not know chapter and verse of the US Foreign Corrupt Practices Act, but they are likely to know it exists. You are probably better off if you refrain from any outraged moralizing, but you can politely explain that this particular Chinese way of doing business is simply not possible for your American company. There is no guarantee you won't lose the deal right there. But you do stand a very real chance of moving right past it with no repercussions.

Many Western business people in China understandably feel powerless to resist the prevailing current of corruption. Adopting a kind of "When in Rome, do as the Romans do" attitude, some allow themselves to be carried along with that current. But David Mahon, managing director of Mahon China Investment Management, Ltd., has warned against the tendency of Westerners to assume that corruption is a built-in part of China's cultural legacy or "some kind of Asian thing" that simply cannot be avoided. "I think it's a function of

China's weak legal system rather than any cultural predisposition," he said. "It is human nature to run wild if constraints are not in place, and that's what tends to happen in China."

There is, of course, a vast gray area between dealings that are squeaky-clean and those that are blatantly corrupt, and it is hard to function in China without drifting into it. Gift giving and lavish entertaining truly are a part of the culture, and for the most highly principled of foreign executives this may sometimes feel like tainted behavior. Upon signing contracts for imported equipment, for example, a Chinese purchasing official may very well insist that the deal include an invitation for a delegation from his organization to take an obviously less-than-necessary "inspection visit" to the provider's factory—especially if it happens to be anywhere near Disney World or Las Vegas! If yielding to such a request troubles you, you can at least take comfort from the fact that the visit is likely to be an eye-opening experience for your esteemed guest, and that China in the long run can only benefit as more and more officials get a firsthand glimpse at the outside world.

Wherever your own limits lie in these murkier areas, the key is to establish them ahead of time in your own mind, communicate them clearly to everyone in your organization, and then stick to them. It's not a foolproof solution, but it offers a real chance to find your way around what may well be China's single greatest pitfall.

Clean behavior by foreign companies can also play a meaningful part in improving the environment. I once heard Hu Shuli, managing editor of *Caijing Magazine,* say that a key to the future development of the Chinese business environment lies in hands of foreign companies, which she urged not to compromise with Chinese corruption. Her appeal, calling on foreign companies to become part of the solution rather than part of the problem, may sound naive. But there is no denying that Western complaints about Chinese corruption will ring hypocritical so long as Western companies are taking part.

OTHER ETHICAL ISSUES

Corruption aside, China poses countless other ethical dilemmas. For one thing, it is undeniable that China pretty much deserves its reputation as a wide-scale violator of human rights. Political and religious repression are real. Of more direct concern to businesses, there are some very serious issues connected to the Chinese labor force.

On paper, Chinese labor law is quite comprehensive, with impressive guarantees of rights covering worker safety, minimum wage levels, overtime provisions, working-hour limitations, and child labor. But in practice, things play out very differently. Chinese labor expert Robert Rosoff has written that "labor rights violations are so widespread in China that violations can be presumed to exist in every factory until proven otherwise."

Would-be Chinese labor activists who seek remedies to these wrongs by organizing workers are usually dealt with promptly by the authorities, and often harshly. Independent unions and the right to strike simply do not exist in China. Prison labor facilities, on the other hand, do.

All of which leads to serious questions about how a Western company can meet its own standards for the treatment of its workers under these conditions. In the case of a foreign business that owns or manages a facility directly, it is a fairly simple matter to implement and maintain the appropriate standards. To do so successfully requires constant supervision, and it will necessarily add to costs in a market full of cutthroat price competition. But it can be done.

Things get trickier when it involves other kinds of relationships. What do you do, for example, if you find out that the light industrial goods you've been buying from a provincial Chinese "factory" are actually made by inmates in a prison or a labor camp? You can choose to tell yourself they are convicted criminals paying their debt to society, and furthermore that they probably *prefer* having something productive to do with their time. But knowing what you do about the capricious and arbitrary nature of the Chinese judicial system, how long can you go without wondering how many of those "workers" arrived at their situation without a fair trial or due process of any kind?

Until the mid-1990s, Chinese businesses that employed inmate labor were not at all shy about saying so, sometimes even in their English-language promotional materials. The practice is seen as perfectly acceptable and not the least bit controversial by most Chinese, and it came as something of a surprise to Chinese officials and business people when they saw Western markets reacting not only with widespread revulsion but also formal prohibitions against the import of goods made under such circumstances. Factories learned quickly enough to keep quiet about the details, shifting into arm's-length subcontracting arrangements that allowed all concerned to claim plausible deniability—including China's central government, which years ago took on bilateral commitments with Washington to block the export of prison-made goods.

But it often takes very little digging to figure out what's going on just below the surface. In summer 2005, the *South China Morning Post,* Hong Kong's leading English-language newspaper, reported that six of the world's largest financial institutions had bought shares in a Chinese wig manufacturer that was using forced labor to make some of its wares. Merrill Lynch, HSBC, ING, and Morgan Stanley were among the banks involved.

Precisely because of its complexity and the intertangled web of involved parties, this story struck me as a great illustration of the kind of fuzzy ethical dilemmas that can emerge while doing business in China. Listed on the Shanghai domestic-share stock exchange, Henan Rebecca Hair Products was China's largest maker of wigs and boasted rising profits. So when China authorized another round of foreign investment into the domestic-share markets, Henan Rebecca was one of many companies to attract interest.

But under China's qualified foreign institutional investor (QFII) scheme, individuals cannot buy domestic shares directly. Instead, large foreign banks that are authorized to buy do so on behalf of their investment clients, and then hold the shares in their names. So where does responsibility actually lie? Like several of the other large banks, HSBC responded by trumpeting its own adherence to exemplary international standards, but refusing to take responsibility for the dealings it facilitates for clients.

HSBC said in a statement that it does weigh the appropriateness of its own direct dealings with organizations and individuals according to high social, ethical, and environmental standards. But, it added, "we would not wish to police the shareholding decision of any third party. This would be undesirable and almost impossible to implement."

As the *South China Morning Post* reporter pointed out in his story, a simple Internet search turned up about a thousand links referencing a connection between Henan Rebecca and forced labor. While it would be foolish to suggest that a 'Net search constitutes any kind of due diligence, those kinds of results do suggest that some proper due diligence might have been in order. But with so many parties at a half remove from the transaction, it seems no one had the incentive—or the desire—to do it.

So where does this leave a foreign business person seeking a Chinese supplier, distributor, or partner? After all, if you look hard enough at any Chinese enterprise, there is a fair chance of spotting something that someone somewhere would find objectionable.

Unfit labor policies may be the most widespread. But what about enterprises that have direct links to the Chinese military, or to those same security forces that chase down dissidents and persecute the millions of faithful who pray in China's underground churches? Other Chinese companies, especially in the energy sector, may be playing a controversial role in China's development of minority regions such as Tibet or Xinjiang.

Some Westerners might very well see serious ethical problems in these situations. But the fact is they are difficult to avoid, and at some point the exercise tips into absurdity. The objective here is not to carry it that far, but instead to illustrate the potential sensitivity of the issues that are in play.

Some major American high-tech companies have been bumping up against these very issues in the past two years—and coming in for some very sharp criticism because of their complicity with strict Chinese regulations on Internet censorship. As widely reported recently in the business and news media, Microsoft, Google, Cisco, and Yahoo! have all grappled with this issue. Microsoft reportedly shut down a blogger whose writings, though fairly tame, had run afoul of the authorities. Meanwhile Google (official corporate motto: "Don't be evil") agreed to filter out search results for users of its Chinese Web site according to the extremely intolerant sensitivities of the Communist party. For years, Cisco has been reported to be providing China with much of the networking technology it needs for filtering, monitoring, and censoring of the Internet. And Yahoo! confirmed reports that it went so far as to turn over the private user information details that Chinese police needed to find, arrest, and convict a Yahoo! user who sent some e-mail that the government didn't like.

With only minor variations, these companies sing a common refrain. China, they say, has its own laws, and while foreign companies may not like them, they have no choice but to abide by them if they wish to operate in the country. That logic holds up well enough on its face, as does the frequently voiced assertion that deepening China's engagement with the rest of the world—on whatever terms—offers the best path forward to eventual liberalization. At the same time, cracks appear in that logic when you consider that Chinese law is far from an absolute and independent construct. Often it is a blunt instrument of control wielded arbitrarily by the state to support its monopoly on power, and readily ignored when that suits its purposes instead.

Even if executives at Yahoo!, Google, or Cisco are not kept awake at night by the ethical implications of their China dealings, they have plenty to worry about in terms of the public relations impact at home and elsewhere in the world. All these companies have come under withering criticism for their actions, and regardless of the other issues involved, they need to take that much into account.

As all these cases make clear, the issue of general ethics in dealing with China can quickly get murky, and unfortunately there are not any facile tips or guidelines to see you through. Ethics is less a pitfall than a pothole that stretches across the full width of the road; there really is no way to skirt it entirely. Instead you have to rely on corporate social responsibility policies and your individual conscience as you tiptoe through. It should at least be easier now that you know it's there.

PICKING YOUR BATTLES

However polite the speeches at a ribbon-cutting ceremony and however flowery the toasts at a signing banquet may be, there is bound to come a time when you and your Chinese counterparts fail to see eye-to-eye. To be fair, this happens often enough in well-regulated Western business environments. But in China, where hardball is played harder, where contracts are less than sacrosanct, and where the legal system is full of holes, it happens even more. I daresay any Westerner who claims to have done business in China without running into problems is either just getting started or telling tall tales.

Small businesses can be especially vulnerable to abusive attempts at strong-arming behavior. As the Chinese side knows all too well, a small Western company is not likely to have much faith in the ability of the Chinese legal system to protect its interests, or be willing to sink much money into legal proceedings.

Paradoxically, though, large companies can be just as vulnerable. And as you'll soon see in a couple of examples, it is precisely *because* of their size that they have less leverage. Whatever your size, it is bound to happen at some point. When it does, you will face a tricky decision about how to respond, and you'll have to pick your battles carefully.

When McDonald's Corporation faced this dilemma in 1994, it decided—wisely, as it turned out—that discretion was the better part of valor. In 1989, just months after the deadly armed assault that ended the massive Tiananmen Square demonstrations, McDonald's signed the deal that brought it into China. It was among the first high-profile deals to follow the political violence, and it marked an important step on China's way back toward normalcy and international engagement. The company got a terrific price on a twenty-year lease for its first store, located just a block away from Tiananmen Square itself. And it also thought it had earned some points with the Chinese authorities for going ahead with the deal during those tense and chaotic days.

But within five years, the company was told the building it occupied would be torn down to make way for a huge new commercial complex, and that its twenty-year lease was effectively void. At first, executives could barely conceal their frustration over this blatant violation of a contract and slap in the face. Other companies took note as well, and began to doubt that China was yet ready to be a reliable business partner.

But it did not take long for McDonald's to reconsider its response. The company already had seven stores in Beijing and nineteen more in other Chinese cities. More importantly, it had plans. Big plans that called for a massive rollout of six hundred more stores over the next ten years. And it quickly realized that an acrimonious legal battle could very well jeopardize those ambitions. It quietly vacated its Beijing flagship store. It signed a new lease for space in the new building and moved ahead full-bore on its expansion plans. Today the company has 770 stores across China, with plans to open 100 new ones each year, and it ranks as one of the best-known foreign brands in the nation.

More recently, some of Germany's top industrial firms faced a similar dilemma, and reached a similar conclusion. Transrapid, a consortium of Siemens AG and ThyssenKrupp AG, had cooperated with authorities in Shanghai in the construction of a state-of-the-art high-speed maglev train line. The German side contributed funding, personnel, and some of its most advanced technology. The eighteen-mile line instantly became one of China's leading prestige projects, not to mention a top Shanghai tourist attraction in its own right. It would also, Transrapid hoped, serve as a demonstration system that might lead to lucrative contracts for a 125-mile extension of that line to the city of Hangzhou and perhaps other lines throughout China.

But the cooperation was soured by allegations of outrageous attempts by the Chinese side to steal the technology. The worst incident occurred at the end of 2004, when Chinese engineers were caught breaking in to a secure engineering room to take measurements of equipment. The incident caused an uproar in German media, with one newspaper reporting that the break-in had even been captured on videotape. Siemens and ThyssenKrupp, though, downplayed the episode.

Just over a year later, China announced that it was preparing to conduct trial runs of its own maglev system, and German media once again railed about an apparent case of blatant technology theft. But yet again, the German companies chose to soft-pedal the issue.

And it is not hard to see why. Siemens has invested billions of dollars across China in dozens of ventures, manufacturing semiconductors, consumer electronics, household appliances, and much more. ThyssenKrupp, meanwhile, is in contention for huge contracts for steel and other commodities. Little wonder executives at these companies would hesitate to antagonize Chinese officials at the highest levels on this case when they have so much else at stake. Still, such a calculation also raises the question asked most succinctly by the German magazine *Der Spiegel:* "To what extent should, can or must German, European and Western companies kowtow to the rising economic power in hopes of generating future business?"

It is a question most Western business people in China will have to grapple with eventually. But retreat is not always the right answer. Consider the case of one small business, run by an Italian woman, Gisa Casarubea, who together with her husband came to China in the mid-1980s to teach. They had always dreamed of running a restaurant, and when their teaching jobs ended they decided to risk their life savings by trying it in Beijing. They partnered with a local man they had considered a friend and poured $100,000 into the venture. Their restaurant opened in 1994 and was well received by both foreign and local diners as a unique alternative to Beijing's hotel-dominated Western food scene.

But they grew increasingly uneasy as their local partner hemmed and hawed over the finalization of the joint-venture formalities he had promised to execute. They also came to find that money belonging to the venture had gone missing, and when they finally confronted him, he admitted that he had been lying to them all along and had never registered the joint venture. In fact, he told them, the lack of the joint venture meant they had no legal standing in China at all: Even their visas had expired, and he had powerful friends among the police and city government. With the flourish of a chess player announcing checkmate, he added that there was nothing they could do but pack their bags and go back home.

They chose to stay and fight. It was a long battle, played out at a time when China's legal system was significantly less responsive and functional than it is now. But finally they prevailed. "Everyone told me [it] was hopeless and that I should just forget about the money and give up," Casarubea told me. Eventually, however, the couple recovered a large portion of their money, which they used to open a small cheese-making business. They later opened another Italian restaurant in Beijing, which continues to operate today.

SENSITIVITY TRAINING

All the talk abroad about China's emergence as an economic superpower is matched by plenty of bluster at home about the nation finally taking its rightful place in the world. But just below the surface there remains a deep vein of insecurity and cultural sensitivity. And many companies have found out the hard way how easy it is to hit a nerve.

Time after time, companies have run into trouble by carelessly offending Chinese political or cultural sensibilities. It happened to Nike in 2004, when it ran a television commercial featuring NBA star LeBron James. Called "Chamber of Fear," the ninety-second spot showed James running rings around a cartoon version of a wizened old Chinese martial arts master. James was also shown vanquishing a pair of Chinese dragons and outmaneuvering a pair of Chinese women in traditional dress.

It may have seemed like a clever and compelling ad to the Nike marketing team, but it caused an uproar in China, where it was denounced as an unacceptable assault on national dignity. Internet chat rooms buzzed with criticism at the way the ad portrayed all the Chinese characters being defeated by the American.

Then the State Administration of Radio, Film and Television stepped in and ordered that the ad be pulled, saying it violated regulations requiring that "all advertisements must uphold national dignity and interest, and respect the motherland's culture." Nike could do nothing but apologize.

A few months earlier, Japan's Toyota Motor had made a similar misstep. The company also had to formally apologize and pull a series of newspaper and magazine ads that showed stone lions, a traditional symbol of Chinese power, bowing down to its Prado Land Cruiser. In another ad deemed offensive by many Chinese, Toyota showed one of its Land Cruisers towing what looked like a Chinese military jeep.

Around the same time, outdoor display ads for another Japanese company, Nippon Paint, also raised hackles. The company tried to show how smooth its product was by portraying a dragon that could not keep its grip on a painted pillar.

In 2006, Kentucky Fried Chicken drew heavy fire when its advertising depicted Fu Qingzhu, a famous Ming dynasty Taoist master, enjoying a chicken sandwich together with his disciples. Critics objected to the appropriation of a revered national figure by a foreign company; some were especially irked because Taoism advocates vegetarianism.

In chapter 3, you read about the excruciating sensitivity surrounding the Taiwan issue. This is another minefield where foreign companies can easily stumble. In 2000 an angry customer in southwest China claimed psychological distress and tried to sue Canon for $12 million when, after buying a printer, he saw Taiwan included as a "country" in a listing of the company's authorized service centers.

Many of the world's largest companies have made the same "mistake" on their Web sites. Audi, Siemens, General Electric, and McDonald's, among others, have been called to task by Chinese authorities for listing Taiwan on drop-down "select country" lists on their corporate sites. In most cases, the companies have backed down by changing their lists to say "select country/region."

While these incidents may seem incredibly petty to Western sensibilities, the reaction they generate on the Chinese side is genuine and telling. Chinese media give them considerable coverage, and Chinese consumers take them seriously. Clearly, Western companies need to take these sensitivities into account as they formulate their advertising and communication strategies.

LOGISTICAL PITFALLS

After navigating the tangle of issues raised by corruption, business ethics, power struggles, and cultural sensitivity, it should be a relative pleasure to grapple with simple, straightforward logistical problems. And in China, there is no shortage of them.

One of the biggest is energy availability. Any company preparing to invest in any sort of industrial enterprise needs to be ready for the possibility of power outages. The risk is of course greatest for energy-intensive operations such as smelters, but outages are also a frequent obstacle for light industrial plants.

In a 2005 report, brokerage CLSA said that 32 percent of small and medium enterprises had seen their electricity supply cut off three days per week. Another 53 percent experienced power cuts one or two days each week.

Foreign-invested enterprises therefore need to follow the lead of Chinese factories, 83 percent of which have their own diesel-powered generators that enable them to keep things moving when the public supply cuts out. But that does not solve the problem entirely, since self-generated power can cost as much as 75 percent more than power bought off the grid. Also, outages often come with no warning, which can lead to production runs ruined in midstream as well as costly equipment damage.

Another tactic is to shift production to off-peak nights and weekends. Labor costs can run higher this way, but power supplies tend to be more reliable.

Water availability is another major concern in any Chinese industrial enterprise. With a natural water endowment far below global norms, China faces an annual supply shortfall of around forty billion tons. Industry and agriculture alike struggle with water scarcity, and that struggle is bound to intensify as rising standards of living raise per capita usage patterns. Already supply cuts are common, especially in water-intensive operations such as power generation.

China's relatively inefficient use of water makes matters worse. According to its own official estimates, the country uses nearly four times more water per unit of economic output than the worldwide average. Its rate of industrial water reusage is likewise poor.

To encourage efficiency and conservation, China has been steadily raising its artificially low water prices, and experts believe it will continue to do so for some time to come. Budget projections of any venture dependent on water must therefore take those rising costs into account.

Price isn't the only issue related to water: Quality can also be a concern. One example described to me is a European-invested water treatment plant in central China that had to cease operations after an upstream release of pollutants altered the pH level of incoming water beyond the plant's ability to process it.

With both power and water, supply disruptions and price turbulence are real threats, and they are largely beyond the control of a foreign company. But advance preparation can at least minimize some of the impact.

KEY POINTS TO REMEMBER FROM CHAPTER 8

1. Corruption ranks as the greatest single pitfall you are likely to encounter when you do business in China. The problem is endemic, and is a major concern both to government and to foreign businesses. You are likely to encounter situations that range

from slightly fishy to downright sleazy, and while you will probably not manage to steer clear entirely, you are better off holding your ground and resisting the temptation to go with the flow.

2. Corruption aside, other ethical pitfalls abound. Western companies can maintain a good degree of control over the treatment of their own workers but need to pay attention to the standards of suppliers and providers. Other prickly issues such as human rights and censorship can also come into play, especially in business done directly with the government. This is inevitable when you choose to do business in a place where values, ethical standards, and the political system are so very different. There are no glib prescriptions for striking the right balance, but never forget that your company's actions in the China market can easily come under public scrutiny at home.

3. Use good judgment in picking your battles. Sooner or later in your China dealings, you are likely to receive pressure or outright abuse, and you may feel the need to push back. Before doing so, you must carefully weigh your chances of success as well as the impact on your full range of interests. Unpalatable though it is, many companies have calculated that it's sometimes better to let things slide.

4. Be aware of the many acute cultural and political sensitivities. The Chinese public can be quick to take offense at perceived insults, and Chinese media can be counted on to play them up. Numerous Western

companies have damaged their standing with their customers by running ads that were meant to be good-natured or fun, but were seen as insulting.

5. Be aware of resource shortages. Just about anywhere in China, your operation may not be able to count on having the power and the water it needs to function. Shortages mean prices are likely to rise, and budget planning should reflect this. Frequent outages mean you need to be prepared with a replacement source—even if that means resorting to a costly self-owned generating system.

Conclusion

My modest goal in the preceding pages has been to give you a balanced picture of the enticing but complex world of doing business in China. Having read this far, you should have a good sense of both the immense promise and the daunting problems you will find if you choose to go there.

Whatever business you are in, you will have no trouble finding a way to get into the game if you want to. You have already seen that some sectors are more freewheeling and open than others, but business people in just about any field will be able to find something to do in China if they care to. As I stressed in the opening pages of the introduction, though, a decision to take the plunge has to be weighed carefully. It is my hope that I have successfully armed you with what you need to know about China so that you can match it up with what you know about your own business in order to make the right call.

The last piece of the puzzle concerns China's future. Considering all the turbulence the nation has experienced—where it has come from and, above all, how much it has changed in the past twenty-five years—it seems an exceedingly risky undertaking to make any guesses about what might come next. Indeed, it would be downright foolish to offer predictions over anything approaching the long term. There are simply too many variables on the domestic, regional, and global levels, both politically and economically, to make any meaningful guesses.

Nevertheless, I *do* believe that certain basic elements of China's near-term trajectory can be predicted with some confidence. And overall, I believe they bode well, both for China and for foreign business.

PROJECTING INTO THE NEXT FEW YEARS

The key point in my mind is that China has finally settled its great debate about what it wants to be and where it wants to go. It is worth remembering that not so long ago, there remained powerful factions within the top leadership who opposed China's transformation toward a market-based economy. Whether out of commitment to the Communist ideals of old, or concern over the intrinsic challenge of keeping political control after letting go of the economy, many influential figures argued all through the 1980s and well into the 1990s that China should resist market reforms and engage with the world economy only cautiously.

But those people have been overtaken by events, and there is now a near-unanimous consensus that China's current path is the right one. There is still plenty of concern over where it will all lead, especially when it comes to the problem of how to care for those who lose out on China's increasingly competitive playing field. There is also plenty of push and pull over how to square today's policies with the most basic tenets of the socialist ideology China still professes to uphold. But there is virtually no one left making a serious case for turning back or changing the basic course. Too many people now have a stake in the current model to make that possible, and anyway everyone understands that the old model could not possibly meet the basic needs, much less the grand expectations, of today's China in today's world.

There is likewise a strong consensus in favor of a strategy based on Chinese cooperation, rather than confrontation, with the United States and other major powers, as well as increased engagement with all the world's great multilateral institutions—for now, at least. There is no telling how disruptive China's rise will eventually be to the world order, but for the near term the country is on course to merge into the global status quo rather than overturn it.

All this has vital implications for the business environment. It means policies will continue to evolve in the direction of greater liberalization and greater access for foreign firms. In some areas, the pace will be maddeningly slow, and this will no doubt hinder the development of certain business opportunities.

In particular, I see three areas where China will be most resistant to change and liberalization: its media, its legal system, and its currency. Together, these form a kind of three-legged stool that the party and government will try to keep in place for as long as possible in the hope that it can bear the stressful forces being unleashed as just about everything else is set loose.

As you read in chapter 5, the government has already lost a vast degree of control over the information people can spread and receive. This will make it all the more determined to keep control where it still has it: the highly regulated state-owned press. However many glossy magazines or Hollywood movies it allows into China, I expect the government will cling desperately to its near monopoly on the control of hard news. For foreign companies working in this area, then, opportunities will present themselves at a much slower pace. More broadly, it means China's modernizing economy will miss out on the potentially beneficial impact that a truly free press could have.

I also see a glass ceiling in terms of how far Chinese legal reforms will be allowed to go. Laws continue to change and improve across the board, and businesses both foreign and local will benefit as they do. But I do not foresee the government ever allowing the law to prevail over its own interests. If so, it is unfortunate, because it means there will never be a true end to all the distortions and inequities produced by a politically dominated legal system.

China's resistance to currency liberalization may be the most difficult to sustain, but that will not keep the nation from trying. Because its exchange rate policies and convertibility restrictions have a direct impact on foreign economies, China is getting pressure from all sides to let the yuan trade more freely. The government clearly remembers the havoc wrought among its neighbors by the 1997 Asian financial crisis, and it desperately fears that a freely traded yuan could expose China to just that kind of instability. But under relentless foreign pressure, China has grudgingly made small moves toward liberalization. Currency may therefore be the first of the stool's three legs to crack. Indeed, by the end of 2006, the yuan-dollar exchange rate began to fluctuate significantly.

Fluctuations will impact you differently, depending on whether you are buying from or selling to China. But for all concerned, greater volatility will make for more difficult planning. It is, of course, something that business people deal with in most other world markets and should be well equipped to handle.

Ideological debates may no longer be a threat to China's progress, but other pressing problems lurk. The government— probably correctly—sees growing inequality as a major concern. Reforms have produced a lot of wealth, but they have also created a social divide between the haves and have-nots. Each year, China sees tens of thousands of incidents of unrest, sometimes quite violent. The causes range from labor disputes to land confiscation, and while the government has managed to keep a lid on things so far, there are real worries about how it will do so if the economic good times come to an end.

To keep its growth rate humming at or near current levels, China will depend in large part on factors beyond its control. Globalization has brought great things to China, but it also means that it will be fully exposed to the effects of a recession in its main markets in Europe and the United States.

Having joined the world, China will also have to keep up with it. Though it has had a magnificent ride thus far, it cannot go on forever as a manufacturing base for products created and designed elsewhere in the world. The government knows this, and has embarked on an all-out campaign to foster innovation. It intends to modernize its science establishment and increase spending on corporate, academic, and governmental R&D programs. It will also seek to incentivize creativity. This will require profound changes in a rote-based education system that fosters conformity rather than innovation, and vast improvements in its intellectual property rights regime.

The stakes are high, because if China fails in any of this, it will not be long before it starts to hear—in the memorable phrase of Ross Perot—"a giant sucking sound as jobs go south." Vietnam, Bangladesh, and Cambodia, among others, are all willing and pretty much able to take those jobs at any time.

China's challenge was best described to me by Dr. Denis Simon, provost of the State University of New York's Levin Institute and a leading Western expert on Chinese science and technology policies. "If China doesn't do this right," he said, "it risks becoming a good twentieth-century industrial economy just when it needs to figure out how to be a twenty-first-century knowledge-based economy."

It remains to be seen just how well China will manage its many challenges, but by virtue of its sheer size and what it has achieved already, it is hard to see it fading entirely from its prominent place in the world. What I said in the introduction to this book bears repeating here: China is and will likely remain central to the functioning of the global economy, and key to the long-term strategies of most of the world's very biggest companies. What is happening in China is probably affecting your business already, and if it isn't yet, it will soon.

By this point, you may well feel that the benefits of doing business in China are hard to discern through the thickets of a complex bureaucracy, shoddy legal system, and distinctive culture, but as I have tried to convey throughout the book, those benefits are real and they are potentially accessible. And despite all the difficulties—which by necessity I have spent a lot of time on here, and you will spend a lot of time on there—the fact remains that what is happening in China truly is remarkable. So a sense of wonder about it all is not entirely out of place. Just bear in mind that a sense of humor might be equally useful, if at times hard to maintain.

The bottom line, though, is that success *is* possible. In 2006, the US–China Business Council released the results of a survey of its member companies. There are fair methodological questions to be raised about this kind of self-reporting, but that caveat notwithstanding, I think the information is worth considering. Of American companies surveyed, 81 percent reported profitability in 2005 for their China operations. Nearly 70 percent said their profitability had increased over that of the previous year, and more than half reported that the profitability of their China operations matched or exceeded their companies' worldwide profit margins.

As for the recipe for such success, the particulars are, of course, unique to China. But the basics really aren't. What it takes is a solid understanding of the environment, which I have tried to deliver in these pages, combined with clear thinking, good planning, a thick skin, and above all a lot of persistence. Good luck!

Acknowledgments

It is a humbling exercise for me to contemplate the vast number of people I have relied upon during my years in China, and the amount of help, guidance, and support they have kindly provided me. And it is a pleasure to take the opportunity to thank them here.

My cousin Elyse Beth Silverberg got me to China in the first place, and while she never imagined it was a role that would last for eighteen years (and counting!), she has been helping me find my bearings ever since I stepped off the train on a sunny Sunday morning in March 1989. I am forever grateful to her and also to Michael Lee, Elaine Silverberg, and Ari B. Lee for their role in getting me to China and keeping me there.

I also owe a huge debt to my immediate family. Not only for making my life in China what it is, but also for their patient understanding during the many months I neglected them over the course of this project. Roberta, Jonathan, Daniel, and Benjamin: I love you and thank you all. Dorothy Lipson also knows how important her love, encouragement, wisdom, and support have been to me.

Marilyn Plafker, Morris Plafker, and Morris Lipson are all gone now, but I never go a day without thinking of them, and remembering all that they have given me.

Nor would this book have been possible without the guidance, support, hard work, and endless patience of Dan Ambrosio, Rick Wolff, Laura Jorstad, Tareth Mitch, and the rest of their team at Warner Business Books. Special thanks also to Scott Seligman, who put us all together and helped make this project happen.

There are countless other people who have taken time and effort (and sometimes considerable risks) to share their knowledge and understanding of China with me. Many others have patiently helped me clarify or streamline my thinking and writing about all the complex issues that China raises. Though I would like to thank them all individually, many will in fact go unnamed here—some because they want or need to go unnamed, and others simply because of inexcusable memory lapses on my part. I apologize in advance to those I may have omitted.

I am also taking this chance to thank some people who know me only slightly, if at all, and who may in fact be surprised to see their names here. These are people whose writings have been especially useful to me over the years, and I did not want to leave unacknowledged their contributions to whatever understanding of China I can lay claim.

Among the many to whom I owe thanks are: Jonathan Anderson, Andrew Beck, Ira Belkin, James Brock, Cao Meiguang, Michelle Chen, Chen Zhiwu, Duncan Clarke, Jerome Cohen, Mark Cohen, Geoffrey Crothall, Dai Qing, John

DeFrancis, Dong Ying, Jeffrey Evans, Jaime FlorCruz, Fu
Zhonggang, Richard Hardiman, Andrew Higgins, Hu Juan-
juan, Hu Shuli, Mansour Javidar, Jia Aimei, John Kamm,
John Kohut, Michael Komesaroff, Misha Krakowsky, Arthur
Kroeber, Daniel Kwan, Willy Wo-Lap Lam, Nicholas Lardy,
Simon Leys, Lawrence Liu, Christopher Lockwood, Stanley
Lubman, Nandani Lynton, Ma Jun, Raymond Ma, David
Mahon, Doug Markel, Paul Markillie, John McAlister,
James McGregor, James Miles, Paul Miller, Robin Munro,
Ken and Lesley Nilsson, Peter Norton, Mark O'Neill, Peng
Dingding, Qiao Gangliang, Stephen Roach, Scott Roberts,
Lester Ross, Andy Rothman, Erwin Sanft, Stuart Schon-
berger, John Schrecker, Frank Siegel, Denis Simon, Joseph
Simone, Andrew Singh, Anne Stevenson-Yang, Jing Ulrich,
Dan Vasella, Wang Canfa, Wang Xiangwei, Jörg Wuttke,
Andy Xie, Zhou Yu, Zhu Hong, Dominic Ziegler.

Bibliography

A daunting volume of worthwhile literature exists on virtually every aspect of China, as well as every period of its history and development. It is a body of literature that continues to grow—not only in volume as worldwide interest in China spreads, but also in breadth, depth, and quality as scholars and analysts gain ever-greater access to previously unavailable sources and materials. Provided here is a listing of titles, including those that I referred to in the course of writing *Doing Business in China,* and others that—for a variety of reasons—I feel are particularly useful, insightful, or important.

Bernstein, Richard, and Ross H. Munro. *The Coming Conflict with China.* Alfred A. Knopf, 1997.

Blackman, Carolyn. *Negotiating China: Case Studies and Strategies.* Allen & Unwin, 1997.

Bond, Michael Harris. *Beyond the Chinese Face: Insights from Psychology.* Oxford University Press, 1991.

Chen, Ming-Jer. *Inside Chinese Business: A Guide for Managers Worldwide.* Harvard Business School Press, 2001.

Clissold, Tim. *Mr. China: A Memoir.* HarperCollins, 2004.

Dai Qing. *The River Dragon Has Come!: The Three Gorges Dam and the Fate of China's Yangtze River and Its People.* M. E. Sharpe, 1998.

Fishman, Ted C. *China, Inc.: How the Rise of the Next Superpower Challenges America and the World.* Scribner, 2005.

Greene, Felix. *A Curtain of Ignorance. China: How America Is Deceived.* Jonathan Cape, 1964.

Gries, Peter Hays. *China's New Nationalism: Pride, Politics, and Diplomacy.* University of California Press, 2004.

Guthrie, Doug. *China and Globalization: The Social, Economic, and Political Tranformation of Chinese Society.* Routledge, 2006.

Harvard Business Review. *HBR on Doing Business in China.* Harvard Business School Press, 2004.

Kynge, James. *China Shakes the World: The Rise of a Hungry Nation.* Weidenfeld & Nicolson, 2006.

Lieberthal, Kenneth. *Governing China: From Revolution Through Reform.* W. W. Norton & Company, 1995.

Lubman, Stanley B. *Bird in a Cage: Legal Reform in China After Mao.* Stanford University Press, 1999.

Mackerras, Colin. *The New Cambridge Handbook of Contemporary China.* Cambridge University Press, 2001.

McGregor, James. *One Billion Customers: Lessons from the Front Lines of Doing Business in China.* Wall Street Journal Books, 2005.

Nathan, Andrew J., and Robert S. Ross. *The Great Wall and the Empty Fortress: China's Search for Security.* W. W. Norton, 1997.

Rosen, Daniel H. *Behind the Open Door: Foreign Enterprises in the Chinese Marketplace.* Institute for International Economics, 1999.

Seligman, Scott D. *Chinese Business Etiquette: A Guide to Protocol, Manners, and Culture in the People's Republic of China.* Warner Books, 1999.

Shenkar, Oded. *The Chinese Century: The Rising Chinese Economy and Its Impact on the Global Economy, the Balance of Power, and Your Job.* Wharton School Publishing, 2004.

Solomon, Richard H. *Chinese Negotiating Behavior: Pursuing Interests Through "Old Friends."* United States Institute of Peace Press, 1999.

Studwell, Joe. *The China Dream: The Elusive Quest for the Greatest Untapped Market on Earth.* Profile Books, 2002.

Wang Hui. *China's New Order: Society, Politics, and Economy in Transition.* Harvard University Press, 2003.

Wint, Guy. *Common Sense About China.* Victor Gollancz, 1960.

Index

About the Author

A New Jersey native, Ted Plafker was born in 1964 and graduated from Wesleyan University in Middletown, Connecticut, with a degree in Russian studies. In the spring of 1989, after a bicycle journey across Europe and into Asia, he found himself in China. He intended to stay there for "a few weeks" before returning to the United States to look for work as a journalist.

But within hours of arriving in Beijing, he met his wife-to-be, businesswoman Roberta Lipson, and before those "few weeks" were up, he was caught up in watching China slip into the massive upheaval of the Tiananmen Square demonstrations and their violent aftermath. He began working as an assistant in the Beijing Bureau of *Time* magazine, and then found opportunities to write about China for a variety of publications including, among many others, Hong Kong's *South China Morning Post,* the *Boston Globe,* the *San Francisco Examiner, Science Magazine,* the *International Herald Tribune,* the *Washington Post,* and *The Economist.*

Within two years of his arrival in Beijing, he was married. Together with Roberta, he has three amazing sons and now, some 950 weeks after arriving, he is still there, and still writing about China. *Doing Business in China* is his first book.

June, 2007
Beijing, China